Asymmetric Warfare for Entrepreneurs

120 Lessons from Lawrence of Arabia

By Luan Hanratty

First edition published in 2011
Second edition published in 2017
© Copyright 2017
Luan Hanratty
The right of Luan Hanratty to be identified as the author of this work has been asserted by him in accordance with the Copyright, Designs and Patents Act 1998. All rights reserved. No reproduction, copy or transmission of this publication may be made without express prior written permission. No paragraph of this publication may be reproduced, copied or transmitted except with express prior written permission or in accordance with the provisions of the Copyright Act 1956 (as amended). Any person who commits any unauthorised act in relation to this publication may be liable to criminal prosecution and civil claims for damage.

Published by Pen Bal Publishing.
penbalmedia.com
Email: luan@penbalmedia.com

Cover designed by Pen Bal Publishing
Cover image is a creative commons image:
"Rub al-Khali desert in Saudi Arabia, Sunset, November 2007" by Javier Blas
CC-BY-SA-3.0
https://commons.wikimedia.org/wiki/File%3ARub_al_khalid_sunset_nov_07.JPG

Paperback ISBN: 9781520853901

To Lesley

Contents

Preface

TE Lawrence — The Ghost in the Machine

I. First Steps — Lessons 1-6

<u>Foundations of Revolt — Précis</u>

1. Learn from Your Superiors
2. Find Like-Minded Peers
3. Exploit Divisions Instead of Uniting People in Contempt
4. Get a Strong Grass Roots Foundation
5. Attack When Your Enemy Is Weak
6. Start Up a Weekly Bulletin

II. Finding a Cause to Fight — Lessons 7-13

<u>The Discovery of Faisal — Précis</u>

7. The Importance of Leadership
8. Pragmatism over Ideology
9. The Limits of Monetary Incentives
10. Take an Unconventional Approach
11. Know Your Own Strengths and Weaknesses
12. Time Your Announcements
13. Embrace a Different Culture

III. Orientation in Your Cause — Lessons 14-25

<u>Opening the Arab Offensive — Précis</u>

14. Demonstrate Versatility and the Hunger to Learn
15. Keep a Cool Head
16. Have a Sense of Perspective
17. Look at the Psychological Make-up of a Leader
18. Stay Logical When Those Around You Are Not
19. Be Aware of Cultural Traits
20. Frustrate the Larger Opponent
21. Minimise the Risks
22. Co-operate with a Powerful Ally
23. Don't Be Afraid to Have a Grand Vision

24. Develop a Good Memory
25. Be Loved and Feared

IV. Developing Leadership Qualities — Lessons 26-52
A Railway Diversion — Précis

26. Put Yourself on the Radar
27. Pioneer New Communications Technology
28. Hearts and Minds are Greater than Materiel
29. Know Your Business and Lead the Field
30. Take the Hard Choices
31. If You Keep Doing What You Are Doing, You Will Keep Getting What You Are Getting
32. Out-Execute Your Problems
33. There Are More Important Things than Market Share
34. Remember the Inventor's Paradox
35. The Intangible Is Greater than the Concrete
36. Divide and Rule
37. The Map Is Not the Territory
38. Practice Makes Perfection
39. Elevate the Individual over the Group
40. Have an Edge in Just One Crucial Area
41. Pride Your Organisation on Intelligence
42. Learn from the Classics
43. Create a Unique Ethos and Propagate It in the Minds of All
44. Metaphysical Weapons are Greater than Physical Ones
45. Be Closer to Your Community than Your Competition
46. Don't Openly Attack Competition
47. Adopt the Pareto Rule
48. Don't Rely on Promises
49. Don't View Cultures in Binary Opposition
50. Take the Time to Crystallise Your Philosophy
51. Use Hardship as a Rite of Passage
52. Use Your Competitor's Strength Against Him

V. Strategies for Competing — Lessons 53-63
Extending to Aqaba — Précis

53. Set the Example
54. Don't Give Up on Lost Causes
55. Be Assertive and Ready for Action

56. Think Big
57. Never Interrupt an Enemy When He Is Making a Mistake
58. Put People off the Scent
59. Don't Despise Your Enemy
60. Intuition Is a Better Judge than the Mind
61. Let Hubris Reign in Your Opponent
62. Hold Firm on Your Strategy
63. Strike From the Least Expected Place

VI. Interpersonal Skills — Lessons 64-78
Marking Time — Précis

64. Encourage Self-Sufficient Independent Units
65. Apply the Milton Model in Communication
66. Engineer Win-Wins to Secure Relationships
67. The Use of Spies
68. Tradition and Continuity Mean Integrity
69. Find Strong Metaphors
70. Pick Your Fights
71. Maximise Incendiary Strikes
72. Give People the Freedom to Do What They Are Good At
73. Value the Unique Individual, Not the Homogeneous Group
74. Let People Fight for Personal Honour and Gain
75. Create a Guerrilla Army
76. Always Think Ahead
77. Don't Take Undue Risks
78. Model and Repeat Successful Behaviour

VII. Handling Adversity — Lessons 79-86
Raid upon the Bridges — Précis

79. Integrate into the Local Community
80. Look for Areas of Complacency in Your Opponent
81. People Smart is Better than Book Smart
82. Live Each Day As If It's Your Last
83. Don't Tolerate In-fighting
84. Put Your House in Good Order
85. Build It, and They Will Come
86. If in Doubt, Bluff Your Way Out

VIII. Changing the Status Quo — Lessons 87-97

<u>The Dead Sea Campaign — Précis</u>

87. Never Complain and Never Explain
88. Don't Let Sentimentality Cloud Your Judgment
89. Make a Name for Yourself
90. Build a Team of Desperadoes
91. Turn Your Team into an Elite Force
92. Foster Internal Competition
93. Turn Enemies into Friends
94. Listen to Customers More than Experts
95. Privately Challenge Established Doctrines
96. Sometimes You Have to Get Out to Come Back In
97. Put yourself in Others' Shoes

IX. Enfranchising People — Lesson 98

<u>The Ruin of High Hope — Précis</u>

98. Treat People as Intelligent Individuals

X. Plans & Aspirations — Lessons 99-110

<u>Balancing for a Last Effort — Précis</u>

99. Don't Be Dismayed by External Indifference
100. Don't Be Weighed Down by Convention in Lieu of True Understanding
101. Ambition May Not Get You There But It Will Get You Close
102. Dress Well
103. Less Is More
104. Play On the Subconscious When Communicating
105. People Are Not Rational
106. Go Beyond the Material Goal
107. What You Think You Will Become, You Will Become
108. Attack the Leadership
109. Develop a Wide Thirst for Learning
110. Leadership Is More About Character than Brains

XI. Personal Growth — Lessons 111-120

<u>The House is Perfected — Précis</u>

111. Stay One Step Ahead of the Pack
112. Keep Flexible
113. If You Ask People Not to Do Something,
They Will Want to Do It
114. Seize the Initiative
115. Collect Information Voraciously
116. Don't Compromise on the Really Important Things
117. Say Yes First and Work Out How to Do It Later
118. True Understanding Comes Only from Experience
119. If You Challenge People, They Grow
120. Say It in Ten Words or Less

Index

Preface

Asymmetric Warfare for Entrepreneurs: 120 Lessons from Lawrence of Arabia is a deconstruction and analysis of TE Lawrence's epic text on warfare, *Seven Pillars of Wisdom: A Triumph* (published in 1926). TE Lawrence was a man of incredible intellect and courage. He was world-renowned in his own lifetime and the account of his leadership during the Arab Revolt is a beautifully-written narrative. The *Seven Pillars* is a showcase of modernist literature articulating ideas lucidly and highlighting the wranglings incessant in the human condition in adversity. It is also a classic military theory, making it the staple handbook for revolutionaries and irregular insurgencies ever since.

To put it simply, asymmetric warfare is where the little guy wins. It is a situation where the insurgent uses his weakness as a strength and exploits his enemy's size and strength as a weakness. This is done to level the playing field and fight on even terms. Learning and utilising this type of conflict is invaluable for entrepreneurs. If we look at firms who are highly dominant in their industries, they have almost always started from positions of obscurity. But they have risen rapidly and taken a stranglehold over the market by being ahead of the curve and being smart in the ways they attack.

The analogy between war and business is a tight one. This book demonstrates how the ancient art of war, in particular guerrilla war, is applicable to the modern world of business, marketing, leadership and negotiation. I have articulated my philosophy of business through Lawrence's philosophy of war. I have also used other revolutionary thinkers including Sun-zi, Machiavelli, Nietzsche, Henry Ford and Richard Branson to elucidate my ideas.

But it is Lawrence who is the real inspiration for the book. He spent two years fighting alongside the Arabs in a side theatre of the First World War lasting from 1916 to 1918. The Arabs were struggling to achieve independence from the Ottoman Empire, which was a 500-year old construct that had become stale and immobile, just as markets do. This was the cue for new players like Lawrence to come in and tear up the rule book.

In addition to this, he was the consummate cross-cultural integrator and a model to any expatriate worker. The following quote regarding the scarcity of water in the desert sums up his exemplary attitude.

> "As my ambition was to avoid comment upon my difference, I copied them, trusting with reason that their physical superiority was not great enough to trap me into serious harm. Actually I only once went ill with thirst."

Lawrence succeeded in such an unlikely environment because he was willing to do the illogical hard stuff in order to be both a good sport and an easy adapter. He was keen to prove that he was a valuable member of the team rather than an inexperienced and inept outsider. He spoke Arabic in various dialects with keen fluidity and at times, for show, behaved more like the locals than they did, even if that was contrary to his western ways. This resulted in seamless integration and complete admiration from his cohorts. He mixed the best of both worlds. He combined his western know-how and education with easy acceptance of different customs and behavioural codes and his pragmatism is an example for all international business people today.

TE Lawrence — The Ghost in the Machine

TE Lawrence was the archetypal revolutionary. He was an enigma and trailblazer quite unlike his peers. An illegitimate child from middle class England, he gained a place at Oxford by sheer dint of his intelligence. Then after graduating and inspired by earlier travellers and ethnographers such as Gertrude Bell and Charles Doughty, he took a post with the Colonial Office in the Middle East where he worked as an archaeologist, studying and mapping the ancient biblical lands which had long fascinated him. During this time Lawrence gained an intimate knowledge of the region and when war broke out in 1916 he was in the perfect position to take a leading role in the Arab uprising against the Ottoman Turks.

Lawrence's job was to act as a bridge between the Imperial British forces based in Cairo and the Arab royalty in Mecca. It was from this toehold that he managed to galvanize and lead the revolt, turning it from a disorganised confederation of tribes into a ruthlessly efficient irregular army. Under Lawrence's stewardship the Arabs harried and hit the Turks until they were completely expelled from the Arabian Peninsula.

Arab success had started as a distant and doubtful flicker of hope. Two years later, the movement had grown in confidence to the point where independence was unquestionably theirs. Likewise Lawrence grew with the revolt. At the age of twenty seven he was a curious dilettante adventurer but as the campaign gathered momentum Lawrence developed a deep realisation and commitment to Arab self determination. By the end of the war he was a hardened guerrilla general, intolerant of weakness and entirely comfortable in leadership. However, the glory was tarnished by a deep sense of guilt over European ambitions to subjugate the Arab world after the conclusion of the war and he never really forgave himself for manipulating them in this way.

Lawrence was a man of intriguing personality. He was persuasive, intelligent, cocky, charming, driven, fair, egotistical, ambitious, scheming, shrewd, proud and quick. But there was a darker side to his character. Lawrence was an existentialist who felt very much constrained by his physical being. He often toyed with the idea of killing himself,

He was a masochist: personally brave to the extreme, caring far more for his men than he did of himself. He loved pain and perhaps he did indeed intend to kill himself when he took his motor cycle out for the last time in 1935. The following passage where he contemplates the futility of life and war embodies his nihilistic attitude.

"To be of the desert was, as they [the Arabs] knew, a doom to wage unending battle with an enemy who was not of the world, nor life, nor anything, but hope itself; and failure seemed God's freedom to mankind. We might only exercise this our freedom by not doing what it lay within our power to do, for then life would belong to us, and we should have mastered it by holding it cheap. Death would seem best of all our works, the last free loyalty within our grasp, our final leisure: and of these two poles, death and life, or, less finally, leisure and subsistence, we should shun subsistence (which was the stuff of life) in all save its faintest degree, and cling close to leisure. Thereby we would serve to promote the not-doing rather than the doing. Some men, there might be, uncreative; whose leisure was barren; but the activity of these would have been material only. To bring forth immaterial things, things creative, partaking of spirit, not of flesh, we must be jealous of spending time or trouble upon physical demands, since in most men the soul grew aged long before the body. Mankind had been no gainer by its drudges.

There could be no honour in a sure success, but much might be wrested from a sure defeat. Omnipotence and the Infinite were our two worthiest foemen, indeed the only ones for a full man to meet, they being monsters of his own spirit's making; and the stoutest enemies were always of the household. In fighting Omnipotence, honour was proudly to throw away the poor resources that we had, and dare Him empty-handed; to be beaten, not merely by more mind, but by its advantage of better tools. To the clear-sighted, failure was the only goal. We must believe, through and through, that there was no victory, except to go down into death fighting and crying for failure itself, calling in excess of despair to Omnipotence to strike harder, that by His very striking He might temper our tortured selves into the weapon of His own ruin."

Lawrence was deeply insightful of religion and history and he was very much inclined to read too much into characters and peoples. He loved to describe races, people and places with inherent characteristics, which is something that seems absurdly prejudiced to our modern sensibilities. But the greater truth is that these vignettes serve a wonderfully imaginative and figurative end in the discourse.

Many have conjectured that Lawrence was homosexual and I think that he probably was but that he fought against it all his life. Homosexuality was a huge taboo in Edwardian society. Nevertheless, Lawrence frequently infers towards it, and his Grecian preoccupation with male beauty is an ongoing stylistic device, in-keeping with his love of poetic physiognomy.

This is the beauty of the text. It is as much a poetic work as it is a manual of military strategy. He manages to fuse these vastly appositive genres with seamless and original style not found since Xenophon — whom he cities as his primary inspiration for the irregular nature of the revolt. The book was a reaction to the standard military theory of the day. He placed his ideas in diametric opposition to the prosaic scientific technicality of Clausewitz, which had long been the unchallenged dogma. History is written by the victors and Lawrence had an acute sense of the significance of what he was doing. He knew that it would echo down the annals of history.

Above all, one thing that shines out from the text is that he was a patriot. He manifested this as a hero and adventurer bar none. He brought down one of the great empires of history, he was adored by the people who knew him and hopefully this book is a fitting tribute to his brilliant mind.

Chapter I

Lessons 1 — 6

First Steps

Foundations of Revolt — Précis

The introductory section gives a fascinating general overview of the Middle East, in particular the wider Arabian Peninsula; its historical and demographic movements, its political environment, cultural traits and the causes of these characteristics. Lawrence possesses profoundly deep insights into the Arab psyche and how, despite their geographical poverty and predicament, the peoples of this region are responsible for producing the great prophets of three of the biggest world religions and countless other religious leaders and thinkers through history.

He discusses Arabia's five hundred-year subjugation at the hand of the Ottomans and relates this to the unravelling situation: crumbling Turkish hegemony against the backdrop of the First World War, the catastrophic Dardanelles campaign and British imperial strength in Asia. At the end of the section he expounds on the delicate intrigues and unfortunate circumstances linking the revolutionary movements in Mecca, Syria, Mesopotamia and the make up of the team of British diplomats and military chiefs based out of Cairo, who are subsequently given the go ahead by London to support the Arab revolution so as to weaken a German ally in Asia. Finally he describes how he used guile and insubordination to extricate himself from this bumbling and stifling bureaucracy in Cairo in order to involve himself in the fledgling revolt — flinging himself into the action where few others dared.

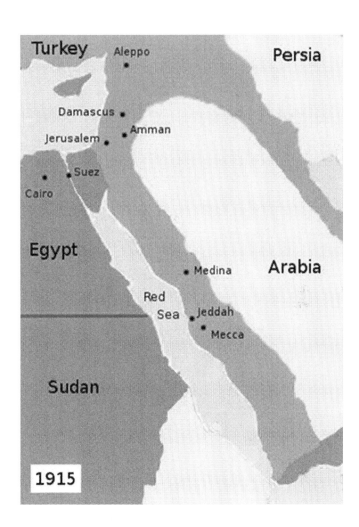

"Some Englishmen, of whom Kitchener was chief, believed that a rebellion of Arabs against Turks would enable England, while fighting Germany, simultaneously to defeat her ally Turkey.

Their knowledge of the nature and power and country of the Arabic-speaking peoples made them think that the issue of such a rebellion would be happy: and indicated its character and method.

So they allowed it to begin, having obtained for it formal assurances of help from the British government. Yet none the less the rebellion of the Sherif of Mecca came to most as a surprise, and found the allies unready. It aroused mixed feelings and made strong friends and strong enemies, amid whose clashing jealousies its affairs began to miscarry."

Lessons 1 — 6

First Steps

1. Learn from Your Superiors

In this opening section Lawrence describes the systematic suppression of Arab culture and nationalism by the Ottoman Turks and how the Arabs responded with defiance in the lead up to the conflict by forming secret societies to plot the downfall of the Empire.

> "The Akhua, the Arab mother society, was publicly dissolved. It was replaced in Mesopotamia by the dangerous Ahad, a very secret brotherhood, limited almost entirely to Arab officers in the Turkish Army, who swore to acquire the military knowledge of their masters, and to turn it against them, in the service of the Arab people, when the moment of rebellion came."

It's very important to take the knowledge which is present in an organisation or in a field and use that information to plan or create something better. We all need people to learn from but at some stage in your career you should be looking to surpass them. It is perfectly natural for leaders to aim to surpass their mentors. Therefore, learn as much as you can from your bosses or other experts but organise yourself independently from them. Nobody has a monopoly on good ideas, knowledge or success, and big ideas are only really worth something if you actualise them for yourself or for your own organisation.

2. Find Like-Minded Peers

In the following quote Lawrence describes the most insidious resistance movement, Fatah; which still exists today as a political party fighting to create a Palestinian state.

> "Greater than the Ahad was the Fetah, the society of freedom in Syria. The landowners, the writers, the doctors, the great public servants linked themselves in this society with a common oath, passwords, signs, a press and a central treasury, to ruin the Turkish Empire. They were deadly secret; and the Government, though it suspected their existence, could find no credible evidence of their leaders or membership."

As the old saying goes, it's not what you know, it's who you know that matters. Networking with other enlightened people in your industry and in other industries is a great way to get ideas and expertise. A similar proverb is that 'birds of a feather flock together' and finding people who share common interests with yourself is much easier today than it has ever been thanks to social media. Usually you don't have to try too hard to find helpful and intelligent friends, you just need to participate socially and you will find people and many areas for mutual co-operation.

The psychologist Carl Jung formulated the concept of synchronicity, which was an attempt to explain the phenomenon of coincidences that seem divinely timed to suit your circumstances. As we will see in Chapter 10, the things that happen around us everyday can really serve as a gift to make our lives more elegant and congruent. If we can tap into synchronicity, especially through social networking, we can increase our productivity exponentially.

3. Exploit Divisions Instead of Uniting People in Contempt

This passage describes the new Turkish regime's heavy-handed attempts at reasserting control over its subject peoples. Their violent response to Arab dissent occurred at the same time as the Armenian Genocide, which began in an almost identical way but concluded in a tragically different result with at least half a million people murdered.

"Mobilization put all power into the hands of those members— Enver, Talaat and Jemal--who were at once the most ruthless, the most logical, and the most ambitious of the Young Turks. They set themselves to stamp out all non-Turkish currents in the State, especially Arab and Armenian nationalism. For the first step they found a specious and convenient weapon in the secret papers of a French Consul in Syria, who left behind him in his Consulate copies of correspondence (about Arab freedom) which had passed between him and an Arab club, not connected with the Fetah but made up of the more talkative and less formidable intelligenzia of the Syrian coast. The Turks, of course, were delighted; for 'colonial' aggression in North Africa had given the French a black reputation in the Arabic-speaking Moslem world; and it served Jemal well to show his co-religionists that these Arab nationalists were infidel enough to prefer France to Turkey.

In Syria, of course, his disclosures had little novelty; but the members of the society were known and respected, if somewhat academic, persons; and their arrest and condemnation, and the crop of deportations, exiles, and executions to which their trial led, moved the country to its depths, and taught the Arabs of the Fetah that if they did not profit by their lesson, the fate of the Armenians would be upon them. The Armenians had been well armed and organized; but their leaders had failed them. They had been disarmed and destroyed piecemeal, the men by massacre, the women and children by being driven and overdriven along the wintry roads into the desert, naked and hungry, the common prey of any passer-by, until death took them. The Young Turks had killed the Armenians, not because they were Christians, but because they were Armenians; and for the same reason they herded Arab Moslems and Arab Christians into the same prison, and hanged them together on the same scaffold. Jemal Pasha united all classes, conditions and creeds in Syria, under pressure of a common misery and peril, and so made a concerted revolt possible."

If you are good at what you do, it is almost impossible not to have enemies of some sort. But as we will see in Lesson 36, successful commanders are realists who find ways to weaken and defeat a larger and more powerful opponent by engineering and exploiting divisions within, to minimise the threat and attract allies where they can.

By killing Arabs, Muslim and Christian alike, the Turks failed to do this. Instead, through their indiscriminate brutality and intimidation they inadvertently galvanised the Arabs — themselves a very fragmented peoples — to unite and rebel in utter indignation.

4. Get a Strong Grass Roots Foundation

Prior to the fight for independence, the Turks had tried to force the Arab leadership in Mecca to comply with the idea of a 'Holy War' against Christianity. Sharif Hussein refused this call and made subsequent appeals to the British for aid.

> "The Turkish demand was, however, not the only one which the Sherif received. In January 1915, Yisin, head of the Mesopotamian officers, Ali Riza, head of the Damascus officers, and Abd el Ghani el Areisi, for the Syrian civilians, sent down to him a concrete proposal for a military mutiny in Syria against the Turks. The oppressed people of Mesopotamia and Syria, the committees of the Ahad and the Fetah, were calling out to him as the Father of the Arabs, the Moslem of Moslems, their greatest prince, their oldest notable, to save them from the sinister designs of Talaat and Jemal.
>
> Hussein, as politician, as prince, as moslem, as modernist, and as nationalist, was forced to listen to their appeal. He sent Feisal, his third son, to Damascus, to discuss their projects as his representative, and to make a report. He sent Ali, his eldest son, to Medina, with orders to raise quietly, on any excuse he pleased, troops from villagers and tribesmen of the Hejaz, and to hold them ready for action if Feisal called. Abdulla, his politic second son, was to sound the British by letter, to learn what would be their attitude towards a possible Arab revolt against Turkey."

Sharif Hussein refused to go against his people. He took a brave position and confronted the overbearing Turkish power, calculating that with foreign assistance and the passive majority support of the local populace he stood a fair chance of winning. In the end he did what was right. Like Sharif Hussein, embattled entrepreneurs also need the help of outsiders and must seek to build strong alliances with powerful firms and institutions.

It was clear that for historical and cultural reasons the defeat of Turkey would be, by necessity, local not foreign. A foreigner should, in the manner of the British General Allenby, enter the country as a friend with the local people actively on his side. Business people entering a new territory also need to build strong ties with the local culture — going with, rather than against, the grain.

A good way to win respect in a new environment is by assisting people where you can with offers of expertise and resources. Being foreign is an asset and carries with it generally positive connotations if you choose to accentuate them correctly. But it can also turn into a handicap if you fail to learn and adapt to the native culture.

5. Attack When Your Enemy Is Weak

Here Lawrence notes the strained situation in 1915 following a diplomatic collapse between the Arabs and Turks.

> "Delay followed, as the Allies went to the Dardanelles, and not to Alexandretta. Feisal went after them to get first-hand knowledge of Gallipoli conditions, since a breakdown of Turkey would be the Arab signal. Then followed stagnation through the months of the Dardanelles campaign. In that slaughter-house the remaining Ottoman first-line army was destroyed. The disaster to Turkey of the accumulated losses was so great that Feisal came back to Syria, judging it a possible moment in which to strike, but found that meanwhile the local situation had become unfavourable."

The Turks were preoccupied with handling another force and that left them open to attack from the South. In business we have to look for unguarded weak spots which our entrenched and stale competition is neglecting and not servicing properly. Others may not recognise these niches but the shrewd entrepreneur must know the market as well as anyone and actively search for the Achilles' heel. Finding such a gap in the market marks the beginning of any great enterprise.

6. Start Up a Weekly Bulletin

Up until late 1916 there had been almost no British assistance to the Arabs. The British had not made sufficient plans and had a generally poor knowledge of the Arab forces, local conditions, resources, tactics and strategies.

> "My private position was not easy. As Staff Captain under Clayton in Sir Archibald Murray's Intelligence Section, I was charged with the 'distribution' of the Turkish Army and the preparation of maps. By natural inclination I had added to them the invention of the Arab Bulletin, a secret weekly record of Middle-Eastern politics; and of necessity Clayton came more and more to need me in the military wing of the Arab Bureau, the tiny intelligence and war staff for foreign affairs, which he was now organizing for McMahon."

Lawrence kept up weekly news round ups on Middle Eastern politics. The Arab Bulletin became invaluable to the intelligence section, the Egyptian high command and to London. Lawrence made a good name for himself this way and soon became indispensable as the British man on the ground, in tune with local details, power dynamics and Arab sentiments. He did this out of duty; ultimately to achieve the goals of the Arab revolt.

A good habit for leaders at all levels to adopt is to send out weekly communiqués to your staff. It bonds the team in unison, gives a sense purpose to your job, allows you to express yourself formally and means that everyone is on the same page as to the company vision. Lawrence had strong and lucid views on matters and he wasn't afraid to air them.

Chapter II

Lessons 7 — 13

Finding a Cause to Fight

The Discovery of Faisal — Précis

Lawrence and his superior, Sir Ronald Storrs, land at Jeddah on the west coast of Arabia in intense heat. They persuade Abdullah, one of the sons of the Sharif of Mecca and leader of the revolt, to agree to a lesser degree of British protection than he would have liked. On talking more with Abdullah, Lawrence develops a distrust of his strategies and his abilities to lead.

Lawrence then travels north from Rabigh to meet with Abdullah's brother, Faisal, who is leading another force. Lawrence is impressed with Faisal and likens him to an armed prophet. At this point Lawrence is requested to wear the Arab headdress and cloak and to journey for hundreds of miles through the gruelling desert to be smuggled into Faisal's camp in Wadi Safra; all under complete secrecy for fear of hostile forces in the area.

At the camp Lawrence observes that Faisal's army is in a dire state; underequipped, ill-rationed, disorganised and on the back foot, having suffered a recent humiliating defeat. But on a positive note he also observes Faisal's striking qualities of personality that place him in Lawrence's mind as the true leader of the disparate and uneasy band of wildmen which made up the revolution.

On the return leg of the trip, Lawrence begins a period of deep reflection and gains a brilliantly astute insight into the situation between the two forces and the reasons for their failures. He concludes that the Arabs by nature are best given to defence rather than attack, being too individualistic and independent to act as a team. From his newly acquired understanding of the nature of the people and their cause, he begins to strategize and make optimistic predictions on the outcome of the war. Upon leaving Faisal, he promises to provide him with further supplies, military support and personnel. Concluding this he begins the journey back to Cairo to take leave, relay his information and unequivocally advise his commanders on the next course of action for the British forces, to which they enthusiastically concur.

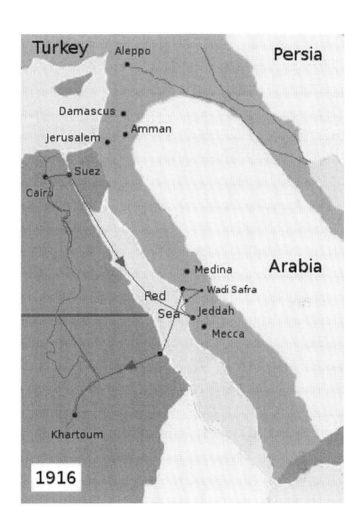

"*I had believed these misfortunes of the revolt to be due mainly to faulty leadership, or rather to the lack of leadership, Arab and English. So I went down to Arabia to see and consider its great men.*

I rode up-country to Feisal, and found in him the leader with the necessary fire, and yet with reason to give effect to our science. His tribesmen seemed sufficient instrument, and his hills to provide natural advantage. So I returned pleased and confident to Egypt, and told my chiefs how Mecca was defended not by the obstacle of Rabegh, but by the flank-threat of Feisal in Jebel Subh

Lessons 7 — 13

Finding a Cause to Fight

7. The Importance of Leadership

After arriving by boat in Jeddah, Lawrence and Storrs are taken to meet the Arab prince and general, Abdullah. Lawrence studies his language and motives with strong scepticism.

> "My suspicion was that its lack was leadership: not intellect, nor judgement, nor political wisdom, but the flame of enthusiasm that would set the desert on fire. My visit was mainly to find the yet-unknown master-spirit of the affair, and measure his capacity to carry the revolt to the goal I had conceived for it."

Lawrence quickly recognises that good leadership is the most crucial factor in a successful campaign. Personal qualities like courage, hope, passion and charisma are always pre-eminent to technical strength, manpower and resources when fighting a crusade against a mighty opponent. We only have to look at George Washington and Simon Bolivar in their wars of independence for evidence for this. A leader in a revolt should possess, in Lawrence's words, a 'singleness of eye and magnetism, devotion and self-sacrifice.'

Lawrence knew his history and history had shown that it is always an 'armed prophet' who succeeds in revolutions. A leader who can inspire the people to do greater things than they had imagined possible is needed in wartime. A cool, calculating or complex leader is more important in peace, attained after the war is won.

8. Pragmatism over Ideology

Lawrence outlines the factors at play behind the Arab Revolt, indicating that the motives for Arab nationalism were overwhelmingly cultural rather than religious.

> "Of religious fanaticism there was little trace. The Sherif refused in round terms to give a religious twist to his rebellion. His fighting creed was nationality. The tribes knew that the Turks were Moslems, and thought that the Germans were probably true friends of Islam. They knew that the British were Christians, and that the British were their allies. In the circumstances, their religion would not have been of much help to them, and they had put it aside. 'Christian fights Christian, so why should not Mohammedans do the same? What we want is a Government which speaks our own language of Arabic and will let us live in peace.'"

In order to achieve their goals the Arab leaders put ideology aside and adopted a more pragmatic and realistic approach. This is not always easy to do and it inevitably meant that the Arab leadership had to question their assumptions about their allies and enemies (British, German and Turkish). Questioning one's assumptions, or at least not putting too much stock in them, leads to uncovering reality and making more rational decisions.

In the Second World War, Hitler turned on Russia at a crucial period because of an overriding belief: his hatred of Communism. In other words, Hitler took his ideology too far and it ruined him. Creeds taken to an extreme are often disastrous and can easily shackle you to a narrow framework of concepts — meaning that you can't see the bigger picture or what's around the corner.

9. The Limits of Monetary Incentives

Prince Faisal's Arab army was a rag-tag bunch of independent fighting men of all ages and tribes. They displayed little discipline but although they could leave at any time, they were immensely loyal to him.

> "The Sherif was feeding not only the fighting men, but their families, and paying two pounds a month for a man, four for a camel. Nothing else would have performed the miracle of keeping a tribal army in the field for five months on end. It was our habit to sneer at Oriental soldiers' love of pay; but the Hejaz campaign was a good example of the limitations of that argument. The Turks were offering great bribes, and obtaining little service--no active service. The Arabs took their money, and gave gratifying assurances in exchange; yet these very tribes would be meanwhile in touch with Feisal, who obtained service for his payment. The Turks cut the throats of their prisoners with knives, as though they were butchering sheep. Feisal offered a reward of a pound a head for prisoners, and had many carried in to him unhurt. He also paid for captured mules or rifles."

Money is a necessary incentive but only when used correctly. Being overly liberal destroys respect for you. Bribes only go so far and do not change men's hearts or their true allegiances. As we will see in Lesson 72, it has been widely observed that giving employees monetary bonuses has its limits. Money is a short term fix and only motivates some of the staff — typically people who are suited to sales. In marketing and in HR policy, throwing cash at a problem is no guarantee of solving it in the long term. In fact, bringing work down to a lowest common denominator of money tends to cheapen it. Vulgar monetary prizes can take away people's pride in the job and tarnish the creative quality of the finished product.

On the other hand, Faisal shows that combining money with giving people increased responsibility is a much more profound and permanent solution, which serves to engender organisational cohesiveness.

10. Take an Unconventional Approach

In spite of Faisal's leadership, the Arab force were not a truly cohesive army in the traditional sense, but a disparate gathering of clans, many of whom had temporarily suspended inter-family feuds for the sake of the rebellion. As a result, their strength in unity could not always be counted on in the heat of battle.

> "One company of Turks firmly entrenched in open country could have defied the entire army of them; and a pitched defeat, with its casualties, would have ended the war by sheer horror."

Lawrence knew it was unthinkable to go into pitched battle against a superior force. He knew what the result would be. Instead, they had to find a radical approach to defeat the enemy.

In business, people are more productive and successful when they think outside the box and approach problems from completely different angles to the way colleagues, competition and customers have always done things. This is true even if it means avoiding them or retreating from situations, just as Faisal was in the process of doing when he met Lawrence for the first time. The ancient Chinese military theorist Sun-zi advocated a similar concept of 'formlessness' to defeat an enemy. To quote from his military treatise *The Art of War,*

> 'Military formation is like water — the form of water is to avoid the high and go to the low, the form of a military force is to avoid the full and attack the empty; the flow of water is determined by the earth, the victory of a military force is determined by the opponent.'

This is the essence of the unconventional fight; allowing a weaker force to divide the stronger and attack on advantageous terms.

11. Know Your Own Strengths and Weaknesses

The Arabs thought and fought along different lines to conventional armies. Lawrence concludes that they were too hard to command, overly reckless and selfish in the pursuit of booty. This made them suitable only in defence rather than in regular attack.

> "A man who could fight well by himself made generally a bad soldier, and these champions seemed to me no material for our drilling; but if we strengthened them by light automatic guns of the Lewis type, to be handled by themselves, they might be capable of holding their hills and serving as an efficient screen behind which we could build up, perhaps at Rabegh, an Arab regular mobile column, capable of meeting a Turkish force (distracted by guerilla warfare) on terms, and of defeating it piecemeal. For such a body of real soldiers no recruits would be forthcoming from Hejaz. It would have to be formed of the heavy unwarlike Syrian and Mesopotamian townsfolk already in our hands, and officered by Arabic-speaking officers trained in the Turkish army, men of the type and history of Aziz el Masri or Maulud. They would eventually finish the war by striking, while the tribesmen skirmished about, and hindered and distracted the Turks by their pin-prick raids."

Lawrence was always planning ahead and weighing up the odds, scouring his mind for possibilities and eventualities. He obviously thought of nothing else night and day. Two of history's finest leadership thinkers encapsulate this behaviour exactly.

> 'A Prince ought to have no other aim or thought, nor select anything else for his study, than war and its rules and discipline; for this is the sole art that belongs to him who rules, and it is of such force that it not only upholds those who are born princes, but it often enables men to rise from a private station to that rank.' ~ Nicolo Machiavelli

Which translates to the business world as,

'I do not believe a man can ever leave his business. He ought to think of it by day and dream of it by night.' ~ Henry Ford

Lawrence was able to visualise the future goal and thus he knew exactly what would be required. He continually judged the nuances of what he saw and weighed them against his ideal. He recognised that disunity in the ranks was not good and that disunited tribesmen would not win the war. He spotted this very early on and shrewdly deemed local tribesman too transient, individualistic and not fit for the task of taking the fight to the Turks conventionally. They were to be utilised however, as defenders or guerrillas, able to launch skirmishes or 'pin prick raids' in the final stages to distract the enemy.

Everyone has a purpose and this is especially true when you have limited resources, and constraints make you learn to squeeze more out of people. In turn, people learn to break out of comfort zones and try new approaches. A key trait of successful people is that they don't complain about the resources they have. Rather, they do everything in their power. They make the best use of resources and improve what they have. The bad workman blames his tools and that is all too easy to do, but the superior worker and manager knows that the world is not perfect. Instead he looks at what he is able to do and maximises the impact of that, knowing that small successes now will bring greater successes and further opportunities to strengthen incrementally.

12. Time Your Announcements

The glaring weakness, which everyone in the Arab army felt, was their lack of artillery. On the last day before departure, Lawrence reveals that the British have shipped over some guns to give them a fighting chance against the Turks.

> "When I told them of the landing of the five-inch howitzers at Rabegh they rejoiced. Such news nearly balanced in their minds the check of their last retreat down Wadi Safra. The guns would be of no real use to them: indeed, it seemed to me that they would do the Arabs positive harm; for their virtues lay in mobility and intelligence, and by giving them guns we hampered their movements and efficiency. Only if we did not give them guns they would quit."

Lawrence knew the value of saying the right things to his men but he only made promises he knew would be kept. This is a huge problem for many managers who make false and even desperate promises to their employees in order to improve morale. Ironically this false rah-rah has the opposite effect in the longterm when the promises don't come to fruition. People have to trust their leaders. Trust is one of the most important factors in the success of an organisation. As evidence of this, the University of California's oft cited research indicates that only 7% of leadership success is attributable to intellect; the other 93% of comes from trust, integrity, authenticity, honesty, creativity, presence, and resilience — all emotional qualities.

Lawrence waited until the end of his visit to give the news of the British armament shipment. He didn't play his cards all at once — although it must have been tempting to do so, arriving as a stranger and unknown quantity. Instead he held his nerve and kept his mouth shut — again demonstrating long-term thinking, good timing and application of emotional intelligence to keep a cool disposition. In this way he engineered respect and a loyal following from the Arab leadership. Again, Machiavelli sums up this attitude in *The Prince*.

> 'And the usual course of affairs is that, as soon as a powerful foreigner enters a country, all the subject states are drawn to him,

moved by the hatred which they feel against the ruling power. So that in respect to these subject states he has not to take any trouble to gain them over to himself, for the whole of them quickly rally to the state which he has acquired there.'

A business person or manager who is new to a place need not try overly hard to gain acceptance from the incumbent staff or consumers. Acceptance will come naturally and more strongly, when combined with a clear and common cause.

13. Embrace a Different Culture

Europeans had travelled and established themselves in tropical and eastern regions for several centuries, and for the last hundred years or so, the British had worn the iconic solar helmet to protect themselves. However, Lawrence as a lone adventurer had no such qualms about adopting Arab clothes and did so for entirely practical reasons.

> "Now as it happened I had been educated in Syria before the war to wear the entire Arab outfit when necessary without strangeness, or sense of being socially compromised. The skirts were a nuisance in running up stairs, but the head-cloth was even convenient in such a climate. So I had accepted it when I rode inland, and must now cling to it under fire of naval disapproval, till some shop should sell me a cap."

Lawrence showed remarkable flexibility in adapting to a foreign cultural climate; something his countrymen had great difficulty with. Entrepreneurs also have to remember that no man is an island and that it is healthy to adapt to your environment.

Stubbornness and sticking to your principles no matter what, is only an asset half of the time. The other half of the time that attitude is unreasonable. The best entrepreneurs are chameleons; culturally literate, not gauche or half hearted, but flexible and sure of themselves. Like Lawrence, business people and leaders must be equally comfortable and urbane both at home and abroad.

Chapter III

Lessons 14 — 25

Orientation in Your Cause

Opening the Arab Offensive — Précis

A month later, Lawrence is whisked back into Arabia only to find that the offensive has been further stalled by another defeat. However, the future is looking more positive as the Turks are being agitated and supplies of weaponry, camels and men come flooding into the bustling new camp at Yanbu on the coast.

Lawrence is asked to meet with Faisal in a town a day's ride away, whereupon he has the opportunity to observe him in more detail. A few days later Lawrence returns to Yanbu to co-ordinate its seaboard defence with the Royal Navy. Then suddenly he receives disastrous news. Faisal has been defeated once more and is now in retreat. The revolt now looks to be on its last legs with many of the tribesmen apparently deserting mid-battle and their artillery proving ineffectual and outdated. With Faisal now returned to the stronghold of Yanbu, they resolve to counter attack by breaking the Turks' line of communications and by pushing sniper parties into the hills to harass the enemy.

That evening, the Navy began arriving in numbers, bristling with artillery, while the occupants of the town dug in and fortified. This show of force created enough apprehension in the Turks to prevent them launching an attack. To Lawrence, this was the psychological turning point in the war.

From this point the Arabs gained experience, confidence and fortitude while their numbers swelled. The next move was for Faisal to capture the northern coastal town of Wajh in a surprise attack while instigating sustained guerrilla strikes on the Turkish positions. Meanwhile, Lawrence marshals the British Red Sea Fleet and organises supplies in support of the attack.

A few days later Faisal's Army receive news that a famous Turkish commander has been captured and that victory is becoming ever surer. Then after taking longer than expected to arrive at Wajh, they discover that the town has just been taken by a British landing party of seamen and local Arab fighters. The revolution gathers unstoppable momentum...

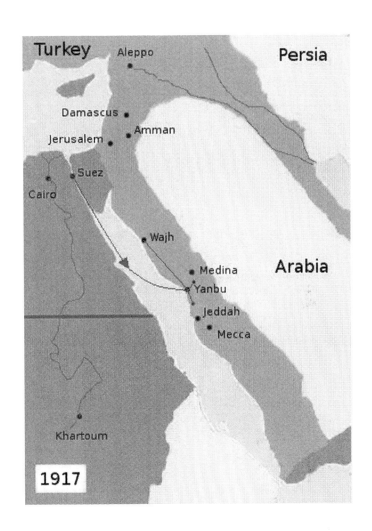

"My chiefs were astonished at such favourable news, but promised help, and meanwhile sent me back, much against my will, into Arabia. I reached Feisal's camp on the day the Turks carried the defences of Jebel Subh. By their so doing the entire basis of my confidence in a tribal war was destroyed.

We havered for a while by Yenbo, hoping to retrieve the position: but the tribesmen proved to be useless for assault, and we saw that if the Revolt was to endure we must invent a new plan of campaign at once.

This was hazardous, as the promised British military experts had not yet arrived. However, we decided that to regain the initiative we must ignore the main body of the enemy, and concentrate far off on his Railway flank. The first step towards this was to move our base to Wejh: which we proceeded to do in the grand manner."

Lessons 14 — 25

Orientation in Your Cause

14. Demonstrate Versatility and the Hunger to Learn

Lawrence was ordered to return to Arabia and begin preparations for directing the war. He desperately tried to avoid this, pleading excuses with his commanding officer General Clayton, but to no avail. They needed to start cooperating with Faisal immediately and could not afford delays.

> "So I had to go; leaving to others the Arab Bulletin I had founded, the maps I wished to draw, and the file of war-changes of the Turkish Army, all fascinating activities in which my training helped me; to take up a role for which I felt no inclination. As our revolt succeeded, onlookers have praised its leadership: but behind the scenes lay all the vices of amateur control, experimental councils, divisions, whimsicality."

Lawrence was the best and most admired type of hero; a reluctant one. He knew that he did not really have the skills and experience to lead an army but he did what all good entrepreneurs do in this situation, he winged it. Despite his shortcomings as a general, Lawrence was versatile, confident and honest with himself. He knew what he did *not* know but he did his best to succeed without complaining or looking for excuses.

A true entrepreneur often has no other choice but to become a jack of all trades, applying himself to diverse aspects of the business and acquiring the skills required to perform every function from sales and marketing to distribution and logistics, accounting, product design and HR. This is best when it is an autodidactic process arising out of necessity which through persistent application and trial and error, the leader ultimately ends up in possession of a rounded and detailed experiential knowledge, so that no crisis can occur in which he can be wrong-footed for long.

15. Keep a Cool Head

Lawrence joins up with Faisal's Army in transit following an earlier skirmish with the Turks. With Faisal's force, numbering around 800 men, they ride for a day until they make camp in a valley thirty miles north-east of Yanbu.

> "We stayed here two days, most of which I spent in Feisal's company, and so got a deeper experience of his method of command, at an interesting season when the morale of his men was suffering heavily from the scare reports brought in, and from the defection of the Northern Harb. Feisal, fighting to make up their lost spirits, did it most surely by lending of his own to everyone within reach. He was accessible to all who stood outside his tent and waited for notice; and he never cut short petitions, even when men came in chorus with their grief in a song of many verses, and sang them around us in the dark. He listened always, and, if he did not settle the case himself, called Sharraf or Faiz to arrange it for him. This extreme patience was a further lesson to me of what native headship in Arabia meant."

Faisal, the archetypal guerrilla commander, demonstrates the strength of his leadership in a time of widespread panic for his army. He sticks to his duties, stays in ready command and deals with even the smallest issues as they arise. In times of crisis good entrepreneurs need to turn and face problems with a sense of perspective rather than panic. They have to stamp out seemingly trivial issues before they get out of control. Leaders do not lose their cool under pressure, for pressure is a time when a cool head is needed most.

In the same vein, the best leaders are the honest ones who always try to understand their customers. This attitude is encapsulated by the following quote from Bill Gates.

> 'Your most unhappy customers are your greatest source of learning.'

This may be hard to swallow but it is true. Marketing people usually prefer to sit around in offices dreaming up conceitedly clever and complex plans, but real marketing is done by getting out and speaking to people. Therefore leaders must always look for ways to be democratic, down to earth, easy going and in tune with the common man. It is the common man who has common sense and the executives holed up in ivory towers don't always see that.

'Common sense is not so common.' ~ Voltaire

16. Have a Sense of Perspective

Lawrence highlights Faisal's calm and friendly disposition despite an embarrassing defeat by the Turks.

> "His self-control seemed equally great. When Mirzuk el Tikheimi, his guest-master, came in from Zeid to explain the shameful story of their rout, Feisal just laughed at him in public and sent him aside to wait while he saw the sheikhs of the Harb and the Ageyl whose carelessness had been mainly responsible for the disaster. These he rallied gently, chaffing them for having done this or that, for having inflicted such losses, or lost so much. Then he called back Mirzuk and lowered the tent-flap: a sign that there was private business to be done. I thought of the meaning of Feisal's name (the sword flashing downward in the stroke) and feared a scene, but he made room for Mirzuk on his carpet, and said, 'Come! tell us more of your 'nights' and marvels of the battle: amuse us.' Mirzuk, a goodlooking, clever lad (a little too sharp-featured) falling into the spirit of the thing, began, in his broad, Ateibi twang, to draw for us wordpictures of young Zeid in flight; of the terror of Ibn Thawab, that famous brigand; and, ultimate disgrace, of how the venerable el Hussein, father of Sherif Ali, the Harithi, had lost his coffee-pots!"

When disasters happen (and they will) charismatic entrepreneurs do not readily lose their temper nor their sense of humour. They appropriate blame but they do it through mild shaming, not through anger. Experienced commanders know that making people lose face can be a bigger motivator than traditional methods of punishment or censure.

Of course there is a fine line between chiding someone to get the best out of them and humiliating them so they greatly resent it and end up hating their work. Instead of making punishment personal, the good leader takes Faisal's course by inspiring the whole team through reference to the organisational goals along with open and objective study of the mistakes that occurred.

17. Look at the Psychological Make-up of a Leader

In camp Faisal kept up an organised and businesslike daily routine.

> "Then till two in the afternoon the curtain of the living tent was down, signifying that Feisal was sleeping, or reading, or doing private business. Afterwards he would sit again in the reception tent till he had finished with all who wanted him. I never saw an Arab leave him dissatisfied or hurt--a tribute to his tact and to his memory; for he seemed never to halt for loss of a fact, nor to stumble over a relationship."

Faisal is never at a loss for words and always in control of the situation. He is hard working, amiable, and able to command faith in people. Like many leaders, Faisal is well organised; making sure he gets enough time to himself without distractions and enough time for necessary interaction with others.

Allowing enough time for reflection everyday is a trait of successful people. A task or project is hard to do well if you are continually being interrupted and losing your flow. Creative people and thinkers tend to explicitly shut themselves away for long periods in the day. This allows you to lose yourself in a complex situation or untangle a problem.

The biggest barrier to this is that in the modern world we feel guilty about giving ourselves downtime. It takes discipline to get away from people, noise and technology but the irony is that those who get more rest and reflect more are often more productive, wealthier and healthier.

18. Stay Logical when Those Around You Are Not

While briefly back in Rabigh Lawrence meets with the French commander, Colonel Bremond. An argument develops as his plan to attack up the coast is met with disapproval by the Colonel, who appears to be less interested in Arab independence than imposing European control over the region.

> "Bremond took refuge in his technical sphere, and assured me, on his honour as a staff-officer, that for Feisal to leave Yenbo and go to Wejh was military suicide; but I saw no force in the arguments which he threw at me volubly; and told him so. It was a curious interview, that, between an old soldier and a young man in fancy dress; and it left a bad taste in my mouth."

Lawrence spots the logical fallacy in the argument. It is an appeal to authority. If people have to use their status to win an argument, they are clearly in the wrong. This is a type of ad hominem or 'to the man' argument and it doesn't hold water. People call on their authority when they are insecure. In which case, the challenger must be sure to never take his eye off logic and facts in the matter, even when dealing with superiors.

Challenging authority is a healthy trait. Most of us are intimidated by authority and people in power tend to abuse it in order to consolidate and increase their beneficial situation. Instances of such selfishness and fuzzy thinking need to be exposed and challenged and nowhere is this more needed and more possible than in the marketplace.

> 'Don't be afraid to challenge the pros, even in their own backyard.'
> ~ Colin Powell

19. Be Aware of Cultural Traits

Lawrence then goes on to outline his reasons for the fundamental differences between the two cultures.

> "The Colonel, like his countrymen, was a realist in love, and war. Even in situations of poetry the French remained incorrigible prosewriters, seeing by the directly-thrown light of reason and understanding, not through the half-closed eye, mistily, by things' essential radiance, in the manner of the imaginative British: so the two races worked ill together on a great undertaking."

Understanding cultural differences is vital to organisational bonding. There is more than a grain of truth in cultural generalisations. British creativity vs continental rationalism is a notable distinction. Typically the Germans and French tend to be noted for their powers of logic, whereas the British are traditionally considered to be more pragmatic and even cunning. This equally poetic description by Winston Churchill represents a similar cultural divide between British and American thinking.

> 'In the military as in the commercial or production spheres the American mind runs naturally to broad, sweeping logical conclusions on the largest scale. It is on these that they build their practical thought and action. They feel that once the foundation has been planned on true comprehensive lines all other stages will follow naturally and almost inevitably. The British mind does not work quite in this way. We do not think that logic and clear-cut principles are necessarily the sole keys to what ought to be done in swiftly changing and indefinable situations. In war particularly we assign a larger importance to opportunism and improvisation seeking rather to live and conquer in accordance with unfolding events than to aspire to dominate it often by fundamental decisions.'

Such broad cultural differences do exist and they are not a bad thing. There is no right or wrong, except in certain circumstances. Cultural traits are there to be exposed or applied where advantageous without pigeon-holing and stereotyping — which is just lazy thinking. If you work in a foreign culture you can observe where holes exist in their work processes and contribute where necessary. Equally, we can all learn from foreign cultures so that what we do at home has an improved quality to it. Great ideas come from overseas and the dynamic exchange and fusion of cultures is what makes the world a more cosmopolitan and prosperous place.

20. Frustrate the Larger Opponent

The attack on Wajh was framed as the most daring operation in living memory. It was calculatingly designed to light the whole of western Arabia in support of the war and to finally put pay to Turkish ambitions, by wrong-footing them to move on the southern town of Rabigh while the Arabs marched in the opposite direction.

> "Lastly, we might develop the sporadic raiding activity of the Harb into conscious operations, to take booty, if possible, in order to be self-supporting; but primarily to lock up large numbers of Turks in defence positions. Zeid agreed to go down to Rabegh to organize similar pin-pricks in the Turks' rear. I gave him letters to the captain of the *Dufferin*, the Yenbo guardship, which would ensure him a quick passage down: for all who knew of the Wejh scheme were agog to help it."

Again, this resonates with Sun-zi's chapter on emptiness and fullness in *The Art of War*. He states that if the enemy is superior, you should demoralise it, distract it and attack its weak points. The Arab tactic was to effectively harry the larger Turkish army with snipers — which the Turks were powerless to resist.

Most industries are dominated by a few behemoth players involved in a cartel-like stalemate of non-price competition involving massive marketing budgets, misallocation of resources and ultimately a lot of waste. These firms get so large that they become impersonal and unresponsive to the real needs of the market. The gaps left by the unwieldy giants are easy targets to exploit for small, nimble and personal service-providers who can play with prices to their own advantage and tear up the status quo.

21. Minimise the Risks

In Yanbu, final preparations are made for the assault on Wajh. Lawrence begins working in close liaison with Captain Boyle of the Royal Navy and the Arab leaders.

> "We agreed that the risk of the fall of Yenbo while we hunted Wejh was great, and that it would be wise to empty it of stores. Boyle gave me an opportunity by signalling that either *Dufferin* or *Hardinge* would be made available for transport. I replied that as difficulties would be severe I preferred *Hardinge*!"

The Arabs took care to spoil the territory somewhat by removing its supplies and enlisting the British Navy, a much needed ally of superior strength, to deprive the enemy of any advantage. The old Roman maxim that 'the enemy of my enemy is my friend' is a win-win scenario for the British and the Arabs and one embodied by this quote.

> 'The best weapon against an enemy is another enemy.' ~ Nietzsche

Like commanders, entrepreneurs have to actively search out powerful friends in their industry. They have to then make formal strategic alliances based on common ground and concrete outcomes. The little player can do this by visualising opportunities and collaborative ideas and by communicating that to the other player — demonstrating intelligence and audacity.

You need to tune in to what your potential ally really wants and then offer it to them in a viable and convincing way. This implies the need for meticulous planning and thought. That is called working smart and it minimises the chances of failure for relatively little extra effort on your part. However, it is also imperative not to gift potential competitors easy resources, ideas, insights and opportunities should the proposal fail.

22. Co-operate with a Powerful Ally

The British and Arabs meet at Faisal's camp to discuss how the Navy were to support and supply the operation.

> "For the attack on Wejh we offered Boyle an Arab landing party of several hundred Harb and Juheina peasantry and freed men, under Saleh ibn Shefia, a negroid boy of good courage (with the faculty of friendliness) who kept his men in reasonable order by conjurations and appeals, and never minded how much his own dignity was outraged by them or by us. Boyle accepted them and decided to put them on another deck of the many-stomached *Hardinge*. They, with the naval party, would land north of the town, where the Turks had no post to block a landing, and whence Wejh and its harbour were best turned.
>
> Boyle would have at least six ships, with fifty guns to occupy the Turks' minds, and a seaplane ship to direct the guns. We would be at Abu Zereibat on the twentieth of the month: at Habban for the *Hardinge*'s water on the twenty-second: and the landing party should go ashore at dawn on the twenty-third, by which time our mounted men would have closed all roads of escape from the town."

The role of the British Navy in the success of the Arab revolt can not be overstressed. Like the embattled but resilient Arabs, crusading entrepreneurs will find themselves in similar positions when entering a market. This is why the previous lesson about fostering allegiances with local enterprises is so valuable. These friendships can provide you with logistical assistance allowing you to utilise their distribution channels, support network, marketing expertise and brand loyalty.

The relationships should be mutually beneficial, in other words you must offer the large enterprise something in return for helping you. An 'I'll scratch your back if you scratch mine' symbiosis is essential for business partnerships to succeed. In negotiations with possible partners always seek out commonality and shared values and goals. Inspire the crusading spirit in your associates no matter how big or powerful they are. Within that common goal there is always something valuable that the smaller party can offer his ally whether it be resources, advice or ideas. You need to show potential partners how you can viably increase their market share and their bottom line through joint schemes at very little or no cost. In that way, everyone's a winner.

'Befriend a distant state while attacking a neighbour.' ~ Chinese proverb, *The Thirty-Six Stratagems*

23. Don't Be Afraid to Have a Grand Vision

Lawrence understands the nature of the situation and the long term prospects a lot better than his superiors and he unnerves them with his positively flippant assessment. He is then privately castigated by Vickery, a gunner with many years experience in Sudan who could speak Arabic perfectly.

> "The news from Rabegh was good; and the Turks had made no attempt to profit by the nakedness of Yenbo. These were our hazards, and when Boyle's wireless set them at rest we were mightily encouraged. Abdulla was almost in Ais: we were half-way to Wejh: the initiative had passed to the Arabs. I was so joyous that for a moment I forgot my self-control, and said exultingly that in a year we would be tapping on the gates of Damascus. A chill came over the feeling in the tent and my hopefulness died. Later, I heard that Vickery had gone to Boyle and vehemently condemned me as a braggart and visionary; but, though the outburst was foolish, it was not an impossible dream, for five months later I was in Damascus, and a year after that I was its *de facto* Governor. Vickery had disappointed me, and I had angered him. He knew I was militarily incompetent and thought me politically absurd. I knew he was the trained soldier our cause needed, and yet he seemed blind to its power. The Arabs nearly made shipwreck through this blindness of European advisers, who would not see that rebellion was not war: indeed, was more of the nature of peace—a national strike perhaps. The conjunction of Semites, an idea, and an armed prophet held illimitable possibilities; in skilled hands it would have been, not Damascus, but Constantinople which was reached in 1918."

Lawrence was ridiculed for his fanciful optimism. He may have been a bit naïve at this stage of his career but he was correct in his convictions. It's necessary to have big ambitions if you are going to lead others and it's actually more realistic to be positive in your outlook than to fear the future. Cynicism is not a healthy attribute. Although it might seem a wiser and more sophisticated line to take, it is actually very limiting and conceited. It stops people from accomplishing what they are truly capable of.

24. Develop a Good Memory

Lawrence recalls with remarkable clarity the march up through the desert on the way to Wajh.

> "The wind had been following our march, and so it was very still and warm at bottom of the valley in lee of the great bank of sand. Here was our water, and here we would halt till the scouts returned from seeking rain-pools in front of us; for so Abd el Kerim, our chief guide, had advised. We rode the four hundred yards across the valley and up the further slopes till we were safe from floods, and there Feisal tapped his camel lightly on the neck till she sank to her knees with a scrape of shingle pushed aside, and settled herself. Hejris spread the carpet for us, and with the other Sherifs we sat and jested while the coffee was made hot."

Both Faisal and Lawrence demonstrate excellent memories in their discussions and observations. Throughout the book Lawrence describes his surroundings with utmost detail despite the fact that his original manuscript was lost and the final draft was completed without notes several years after the war. Lawrence's descriptions of the desert contain some amazing observations especially in regards to the geographical nature of the region and the terrain he, his men and their camels traversed. His descriptions most probably contain some artistic license, but nevertheless, the extensive narrative is impressive in its exactness and allows us inside an exceptionally erudite and lucid mind.

Business leaders too must possess excellent memories in order to retain facts, and keep to promises that they or others have made. Memory is something that, although many profess to having a weakness in, everyone can improve consciously. Business people with good memories succeed where others fail. They pick up on things and recall ideas that ultimately win deals and increase the profitability of the company. A good memory improves judgement in negotiations so you are better informed to take a strong position or in deciding to walk away from the table. A good memory turns intangible truths into tangible assets and lessens the chance making of bad choices.

25. Be Loved and Feared

After Wajh was captured many of the men went on a looting spree. Faisal responded with severity.

> "He brought in his rough-riders and in one day of wholesale arrest and summary punishment persuaded everyone to leave things alone. After that Wejh had the silence of fear."

Straight out of Machiavelli's *Prince*, Faisal is both loved and feared by his men. He knows that fear is the primary of these two qualities and responds to insurrection accordingly. When the men begin to rape and pillage the town he nips it in the bud and dispenses the necessary severe reprisals in one swift swoop.

We saw in Lesson 16 how Faisal used face loss rather than force to punish his men. Face loss is a form of fear, just as a corporal punishment is. The reason Machiavelli promoted fear above love is that fear is the more reliable of the two motivators. This is because love concerns what other people receive from your generosity whereas fear is about what can be taken from you. Humans are essentially selfish beings and therefore always place their own standing above that which they can confer on others.

The good manager must be aware of this and understand that people don't always do what is right out of their own volition but out of factors which imply their own benefit somewhere along the line. Fear has the ability to constrain bad behaviour whereas love has no such power to stop it from being broken as soon as necessary circumstances arise in which it appears necessary to break it.

Chapter IV

Lessons 26 — 52

Developing Leadership Qualities

A Railway Diversion — Précis

With the recent success, the revolution had gained much admiration and support from Lawrence's superiors in Cairo. Back in Wajh Faisal's base became settled, British cars and motorcycles arrive and the Navy help to set up a wireless communications network. The next target was now the holy city of Medina which lay inland to the south east. The Turks had committed a large proportion of their forces to defending the Hejaz Railway and so the Arabs, seizing the initiative, set about sabotaging this valuable yet vulnerable piece of infrastructure. In addition, the cause had further secured the allegiance of many powerful warlords who guaranteed security and armed assistance in expanding the front to the north with the overall aim of taking Aqaba and laying the way for eventually entering Damascus as victors. One of the most famous and senior of the chieftains was Auda, who was according to Lawrence, the greatest fighting man in northern Arabia.

Meanwhile, news comes from an intercepted telegraph message from the Turkish and German high command in Constantinople, ordering the Turkish force in Medina to withdraw. The Allied forces don't want this to happen so they send Lawrence to persuade the Arabs to attack Medina immediately, to which Faisal agrees. The Arabs begin mobilising to prevent the now incipient Turkish evacuation.

Lawrence then sets out in search of Faisal's brother and subordinate general, Abdullah. By this time the narrator is suffering a heavy fever brought on by dysentery and having to endure a long and painful yet beautiful and vivid journey through the desert. After reaching Abdullah and delivering Faisal's plan, Lawrence, completely exhausted and immobile, begins to mull over the campaign, attempting and failing to reconcile the revolt with his well-versed knowledge of orthodox military theory. He concludes that the attack on Medina is a risky and pointless exercise and that the better ploy would be to allow the Turks to stay there and starve themselves out. Lawrence eventually comes to the realisation that with 99.9 per cent of the territory in Arab hands, the war was already won. His rejection of total annihilation of the enemy is particularly revelationary when contrasted with the futility and unchallenged idiocy of what was happening in the European theatre at this time.

Understanding that he himself is in de facto command of the revolt, upon recovery he immediately gathers men, guns and explosives to go and attack the railway. After a long ride they spot the line and a small Turkish camp from a hilltop. In the middle of the night they venture out to blow the line in two places so as to trap the visiting train. They then assail the garrison with gunfire. The assault was successful in wrecking the camp but the train got away. They continued creating havoc into the following day with a new heavy-duty mine laid on the track and much terrorising of the enemy's positions. The Allies now fully grasped the idea that planting mines was the only way to destroy the Turks' railway and their morale.

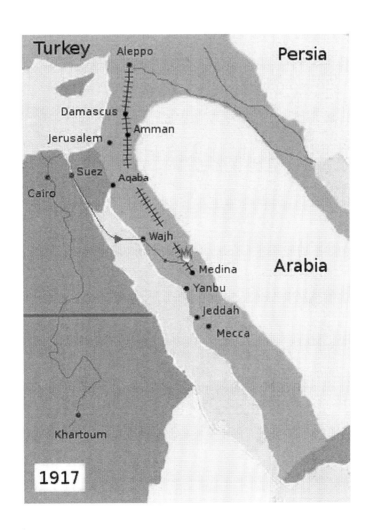

"Our taking Wejh had the wished effect upon the Turks, who abandoned their advance towards Mecca for a passive defence of Medina and its railway. Our experts made plans for attacking them.

The Germans saw the danger of envelopment, and persuaded Enver to order the instant evacuation of Medina. Sir Archibald Murray begged us to put in a sustained attack to destroy the retreating enemy.

Feisal was soon ready in his part: and I went off to Abdulla to get his co-operation. On the way I fell sick and while lying alone with empty hands was driven to think about the campaign. Thinking convinced me that our recent practice had been better than our theory.

So on recovery I did little to the railway, but went back to Wejh with novel ideas. I tried to make the others admit them, and adopt deployment as our ruling principle; and to put preaching even before fighting. They preferred the limited and direct objective of Medina. So I decided to slip off to Akaba by myself on test of my own theory."

Lessons 26 — 52

Developing Leadership Qualities

26. Put Yourself on the Radar

Spirits are high back in Cairo as the campaign appears to be going better than expected.

"In Cairo were Hogarth and George Lloyd, and Storrs and Deedes, and many old friends. Beyond them the circle of Arabian wellwishers was now strangely increased. In the army our shares rose as we showed profits. Lynden Bell stood firmly our friend and swore that method was coming out of the Arab madness. Sir Archibald Murray realized with a sudden shock that more Turkish troops were fighting the Arabs than were fighting him, and began to remember how he had always favoured the Arab revolt. Admiral Wemyss was as ready to help now as he had been in our hard days round Rabegh. Sir Reginald Wingate, High Commissioner in Egypt, was happy in the success of the work he had advocated for years. I grudged him this happiness; for McMahon, who took the actual risk of starting it, had been broken just before prosperity began. However, that was hardly Wingate's fault.

In the midst of my touching the slender stops of all these quills there came a rude surprise. Colonel Bremond called to felicitate me on the capture of Wejh, saying that it confirmed his belief in my military talent and encouraged him to expect my help in an extension of our success. He wanted to occupy Akaba with an Anglo-French force and naval help. He pointed out the importance of Akaba, the only Turkish port left in the Red Sea, the nearest to the Suez Canal, the nearest to the Hejaz Railway, on the left flank of the Beersheba army; suggesting its occupation by a composite brigade, which should advance up Wadi Itm for a crushing blow at Maan. He began to enlarge on the nature of the ground."

As a young man in his twenties, Lawrence was eager to escape a stuffy office environment in Cairo and seek out the action. His sense of adventure, ambition and romantic ideals are a lesson to all young people embarking on a fulfilling and successful business career. If you take the right type of risks and be quick to volunteer for projects, the fruits you bear both in recognition and experience will be worth ten-fold in the long run. Bosses love to see a person who can take responsibility and think for themselves, because it shows that they are committed, proactive and initiative driven.

If you are starting off on the career ladder it is often a good idea to be prepared to work for very little or even nothing in an industry that you love. You don't have the power to choose what you are given, but you do have to the power to choose what you love. Again, bosses love to see this. It shows that you understand how business works. That is, it's not about MBAs, it's about enthusiasm and knowing what's happening around you. It's about being prepared to get your hands dirty and take a stake in the daily functioning of the company. Even if this means making tea or running errands for people, if you stick around and make yourself known as the go-to-guy who's a quick learner with a friendly attitude, you will find yourself hired in full-time post. Permanent jobs can always be found for people like this.

27. Pioneer New Communications Technology

The camp at Wajh develops a vibrant spirit as support comes in from the British, including motor bikes, two Rolls Royce armoured cars and a radio station.

> "The Navy added greatly to our interests in Wejh. The *Espiegle* was sent by Boyle as station ship, with the delightful orders to 'do everything in her power to co-operate in the many plans which would be suggested to her by Colonel Newcombe, while letting it be clearly seen that she was conferring a favour'. Her commander Fitzmaurice (a good name in Turkey), was the soul of hospitality and found quiet amusement in our work on shore. He helped us in a thousand ways; above all in signalling; for he was a wireless expert, and one day at noon the *Northbrook* came in and landed an army wireless set, on a light lorry, for us. As there was no one to explain it, we were at a loss; but Fitzmaurice raced ashore with half his crew, ran the car to a fitting site, rigged the masts professionally, started the engine, and connected up to such effect that before sunset he had called the astonished *Northbrcok* and held a long conversation with her operator. The station increased the efficiency of the base at Wejh and was busy day and night, filling the Red Sea with messages in three tongues, and twenty different sorts of army cypher-codes."

The importance of communication especially in utilising the infrastructure and networks of your allies is crucial. Communications give you a distinct strategic advantage and exploiting new modes keeps costs low and keeps you ahead of the curve. The internet has made it possible for individuals to punch above their weight on a global scale and challenge the dominant players on a level playing field. Social networking has meant that any small business can forge a strong presence and large following and can directly interact with customers around the world at no cost. Blogging means people can publish their thoughts, present marketing copy and demonstrate talent instantly and without the many barriers and shortcomings which exist with traditional print media. This democratisation of society through digital media means that asymmetric entrepreneurs have more opportunities than ever before.

28. Hearts and Minds are Greater than Materiel

As the Turks fail to respond, preferring to hold Medina, Faisal consolidates his power over Western Arabia.

> "He could now prepare to deal solemnly with the Hejaz Railway; but with a practice better than my principles, I begged him first to delay in Wejh and set marching an intense movement among the tribes beyond us, that in the future our revolt might be extended, and the railway threatened from Tebuk (our present limit of influence) northward as far as Maan. My vision of the course of the Arab war was still purblind. I had not seen that the preaching was victory and the fighting a delusion. For the moment, I roped them together, and, as Feisal fortunately liked changing men's minds rather than breaking railways, the preaching went the better."

Lawrence did not wish to completely break the railway. In the long run it wouldn't have done their cause any good, as the Turks would have evacuated and regrouped in stronger positions elsewhere making them harder to root out.

Machiavelli wrote that when a ruler has more to fear from a foreign force than he has from his own people, he should destroy the castles in his territory. If on the other hand, he has something to fear from the people, then he should build and maintain castles. Ultimately he believed that the best fortress of all is not to be hated by the people.

The railway is a similar infrastructure of control and the same lesson applies. The Arabs, fighting a foreign power, needed to damage the sections of the railway in their territory to render it inoperable, causing difficulty and discomfort for the Turks. But in order to keep the enemy vulnerable and bogged down, they did not break it altogether. Rather than razing their castle, they kept it open and ramshackled to create even more weakness and pain.

The point is that the insurgent marketer knows that large amounts of floor space, equipment, fancy materials and conventional infrastructure carry with them proportionate levels of investment, management, risk and cost. All this when a more efficient means of doing business can be maximised through:

- the competition remaining relatively disabled in their modes
- putting the onus on fighting a campaign of ideas and surprises
- enjoying the convenience and flexibility provided by an ethereal yet popular presence

29. Know Your Business and Lead the Field

Supporters including many tribal leaders start flooding in from all corners of northern and western Arabia. Faisal welcomes them all.

> During two years Feisal so laboured daily, putting together and arranging in their natural order the innumerable tiny pieces which made up Arabian society, and combining them into his one design of war against the Turks. There was no blood feud left active in any of the districts through which he had passed, and he was Court of Appeal, ultimate and unchallenged, for western Arabia.
>
> He showed himself worthy of this achievement. He never gave a partial decision, nor a decision so impracticably just that it must lead to disorder. No Arab ever impugned his judgements, or questioned his wisdom and competence in tribal business. By patiently sifting out right and wrong, by his tact, his wonderful memory, he gained authority over the nomads from Medina to Damascus and beyond. He was recognized as a force transcending tribe, superseding blood chiefs, greater than jealousies.

If you are a leader or wish to be one, you can't expect anyone to work harder or know more about the business than you do. The best leaders, like Faisal, have an eye for detail and they do their homework on every issue so they don't give out mixed or muddled messages. To the best leader, every matter has a simple, straight answer. They can do this because they genuinely understand the facts involved. They know everything about every process and every person involved in the business. They instigate a meritocracy and they keep on top of the game.

30. Take the Hard Choices

On his way to meet Abdullah in Wadi Ais, two members of Lawrence's travelling party get into a quarrel whereby Hamed, a Moor, shoots and kills one of the Arabs. Lawrence decides that the responsibility to exact punishment lies with himself.

> "Then rose up the horror which would make civilized man shun justice like a plague if he had not the needy to serve him as hangmen for wages. There were other Moroccans in our army; and to let the Ageyl kill one in feud meant reprisals by which our unity would have been endangered. It must be a formal execution, and at last, desperately, I told Hamed that he must die for punishment, and laid the burden of his killing on myself. Perhaps they would count me not qualified for feud. At least no revenge could lie against my followers; for I was a stranger and kinless."

Entrepreneurs can't shy away from difficult decisions and actions. Strong individuals take a stand. They are prepared to go against the grain and to take the road less travelled. In life and in business, doing things the hard way is often the right way to do things. If you demonstrate this then you set yourself apart from the crowd.

Inevitably managers have to fire ill-behaved employees and assert unpopular policies. Doing this is difficult. It takes courage. Ernest Hemingway described courage as 'grace under pressure' and although difficult decisions can be unpleasant, outwardly you have to show cool and unshaking resolve. Leaders like Lawrence do this by reminding themselves and articulating their reasons; that in doing the dirty work, they are doing it for the greater good.

31. If You Keep Doing What You Are Doing, You Will Keep Getting What You Are Getting

As Lawrence recovers from his fever in Abdullah's camp, his wits return and he begins to examine the progress of the war. It dawns on him that the military orthodoxy everyone was blindly adhering to is not applicable to their struggle.

> "... for we were indubitably winning our war; and as I pondered slowly, it dawned on me that we had won the Hejaz war. Out of every thousand square miles of Hejaz nine hundred and ninety-nine were now free. Did my provoked jape at Vickery, that rebellion was more like peace than like war, hold as much truth as haste? Perhaps in war the absolute did rule, but for peace a majority was good enough. If we held the rest, the Turks were welcome to the tiny fraction on which they stood, till peace or Doomsday showed them the futility of clinging to our window-pane."

The phrase 'If you keep doing what you are doing, you will keep getting what you are getting' is one of the central presuppositions of Neuro-Linguistic Programming (NLP). If there are areas of your life or business which you are not happy with then the fact is that you have to change something fundamental right now if you ever hope to get a different result.

This is also true for the good things that happen. As the old proverb states, 'If something is not broken, then don't fix it.' This is often overlooked by people who wish to meddle with processes which are largely getting the best results to be expected. Tweaking processes is fine and indeed necessary but wrecking good opportunities comes from over-management and lack of understanding. Sometimes the best policy once you have a largely successful process or product is just to keep going and not fret with unrealistic and impractical worries and expectations.

32. Out-Execute Your Problems

Lawrence further ponders the shortcomings of the classical doctrines of war expounded by Clausewitz and Foch, the 19th century's dominant military theorists.

> "Often the parties did not know their aim, and blundered till the march of events took control. Victory in general habit leaned to the clear-sighted, though fortune and superior intelligence could make a sad muddle of nature's 'inexorable' law."

You can't legislate for every eventuality. Unexpected problems are guaranteed to happen but you can control your reaction to those problems. Even if you have planned in great detail and you realise you were mistaken in your initial choices, whether that be a product design, an advertising campaign, a bad purchase or a difficult industry with too many competitors, always remember that you can still out-execute tough competition and circumstances to make the best of a bad situation.

We can succeed in adversity by working even harder and making smarter and more holistic decisions so that consecutively they amplify into a desirable end result. In established companies you often don't have the freedom to execute. But the little guy, the start up worker, has that ability, scope and unity of purpose.

> "The difference between a good business and a bad business is that good businesses throw up one easy decision after another. The bad businesses throw up painful decisions time after time." ~ Charlie Munger

33. There Are More Important Things Than Market Share

Alternatively, if the Arabs could work towards a non-violent and simpler end to the situation, they would without question, take it.

> "I wondered why Feisal wanted to fight the Turks, and why the Arabs helped him, and saw that their aim was geographical, to extrude the Turk from all Arabic-speaking lands in Asia. Their peace ideal of liberty could exercise itself only so. In pursuit of the ideal conditions we might kill Turks, because we disliked them very much; but the killing was a pure luxury. If they would go quietly the war would end. If not, we would urge them, or try to drive them out. In the last resort, we should be compelled to the desperate course of blood and the maxims of 'murder war', but as cheaply as could be for ourselves, since the Arabs fought for freedom, and that was a pleasure to be tasted only by a man alive. Posterity was a chilly thing to work for, no matter how much a man happened to love his own, or other people's already-produced children."

This resonates with the myth that market share is the holy grail of business. The truth is that, just as liberty is the real goal of the war, profit is the true goal of a business. Driving the Turks out of the whole territory would be a nice satisfying and visible achievement but it's not of primary importance, nor is it practically possible. Dominating market share may sound impressive when talking to clients, staff or shareholders but it's largely a secondary aim.

Many of the greatest companies in the world are niche businesses and always have been. The true lifeblood of a successful business is profitability, cash flow, innovation, future growth. Market share is more about praising the status quo — it is transitory, temporal and there is no way of proving how big a company's market share really is. Market share is a competitor not a goal.

34. Remember the Inventor's Paradox

After speaking to Abdullah and becoming more sure of the flaws of traditional war in the Arab context, Lawrence tries to build a new coherent theory of his own.

> "When it grew too hot for dreamless dozing, I picked up my tangle again, and went on ravelling it out, considering now the whole house of war in its structural aspect, which was strategy, in its arrangements, which were tactics, and in the sentiment of its inhabitants, which was psychology; for my personal duty was command, and the commander, like the master architect, was responsible for all."

Look at your business and its issues from the most fundamental points. The only thing that all difficult problems need is time. Time solves all. The problem is that people rarely give themselves enough time to think deeply about the issues.

There are basically two ways to think a problem through; one conscious, the other subconscious. Most of us are practised at the conscious process of focussing directly on something until, if you're lucky, the solution comes. But the inventor's paradox states that you solve a specific problem by solving a more general problem. The moon landing is a good example of something that seemed impossible at first but when reframed in a general perspective became much easier to break down into smaller processes.

When untangling situations it is conducive to take time out and think about nothing in particular until you begin to see the bigger context surrounding the situation. As mentioned in Lesson 17, one of the best ways to do this is to give yourself proper amounts of time everyday to meditate in silence just as Lawrence did. It's not always easy to pull yourself away from the world, but it means you can ultimately think more clearly, stay more relaxed and make your life more organised. A problem or a decision which may seem insurmountable often disappears when you sleep on it — the solution becomes clear cut. This is because your subconscious, during the stages of REM sleep, has had time to piece together the jigsaw that is your life and defragment your mind.

35. The Intangible is Greater than the Concrete

Lawrence continues to visualise the situation on a scientific level. Then the solution suddenly strikes him.

> "I began idly to calculate how many square miles: sixty: eighty: one hundred: perhaps one hundred and forty thousand square miles. And how would the Turks defend all that? No doubt by a trench line across the bottom, if we came like an army with banners; but suppose we were (as we might be) an influence, an idea, a thing intangible, invulnerable, without front or back, drifting about like a gas? Armies were like plants, immobile, firm-rooted, nourished through long stems to the head. We might be a vapour, blowing where we listed. Our kingdoms lay in each man's mind; and as we wanted nothing material to live on, so we might offer nothing material to the killing. It seemed a regular soldier might be helpless without a target, owning only what he sat on, and subjugating only what, by order, he could poke his rifle at."

This is the true crux of Lawrence's philosophy of guerrilla warfare. Such formlessness is why the Taliban remained an elusive and unbeatable force in Afghanistan despite the technology, manpower and money of the American military. Small companies can and must employ this ethos in their operations so they can outwit and fight on level terms with far bigger competition.

Winston Churchill, contemplating the new post-war world order in his 1943 speech at Harvard said that 'The empires of the future are the empires of the mind.' In a modern world, no longer are the physical infrastructures and tools of former times enough to succeed. Instead, ideologies and ethereal metaphysical qualities like knowledge, education and emotional intelligence must be harnessed. Persuasion of the human mind is a greater force than power over the body. Smallness can be an advantage and the power to preach a different story can be enough to gain the support and custom needed to win in any market place.

The idea of strength in smallness and Lawrence's description of the enemy as plants resonates strongly with this empirical metaphor by Peter Drucker, one of the first modern management thinkers.

'An organization, a social artifact, is very different from a biological organism. Yet it stands under the law that governs the structure of animals and plants: The surface goes up with the square of the radius, but the mass grows with the cube. The larger the animal becomes, the more resources have to be devoted to the mass and to the internal tasks, to circulation and information, to the nervous system, and so on.

Every part of an amoeba is in constant direct contact with the environment. It therefore needs no special organs to perceive its environment or to hold it together. But a large and complex animal such as a man needs a skeleton to hold it together. It needs all kinds of specialized organs for ingestion and digestion, for respiration and exhalation, for carrying oxygen to the tissues, for reproduction, and so on. Above all, a man needs a brain and a number of complex nervous systems. Most of the mass of the amoeba is directly concerned with survival and procreation. Most of the mass of the higher animal — its resources, its food, its energy supply, its tissues — serve to overcome and offset the complexity of the structure and isolation from the outside.

An organization is not, like an animal, an end in itself, and successful by the mere act of perpetuating the species. An organization is an organ of society and fulfills itself by the contribution it makes to the outside environment. And yet the bigger and apparently more successful an organization gets to be, the more will inside events tend to engage the interests, the energies, and the abilities of the executive to the exclusion of his real tasks and his real effectiveness in the outside.'

Small organisms have a big advantage over large ones. They can focus on the realities of their environment without having to take care of too many internal processes. Intangible means such as: smart communications, quality ideas, surprise, strong beliefs and clever principles, pricing strategy, excellent service and word of mouth are more powerful than infrastructure, money, drone-like workforces, distribution networks and established presence. This means that the small firm can overcome competitors with big resources at their disposal. Small firms can constantly observe and adapt to the market while large firms remain inward-looking and slow.

36. Divide and Rule

Lawrence realises that the Turks couldn't hope to hold the land against a passively hostile native majority combined with an agitating minority of guerrillas.

> "Then I figured out how many men they would need to sit on all this ground, to save it from our attack-in-depth, sedition putting up her head in every unoccupied one of those hundred thousand square miles. I knew the Turkish Army exactly, and even allowing for their recent extension of faculty by aeroplanes and guns and armoured trains (which made the earth a smaller battlefield) still it seemed they would have need of a fortified post every four square miles, and a post could not be less than twenty men. If so, they would need six hundred thousand men to meet the ill-wills of all the Arab peoples, combined with the active hostility of a few zealots."

The natural state of large markets is that they come to be dominated by several big players who then become lazy and greedy. In this equilibrium state of monopolistic competition, they converge towards homogeneity and neglect the demands of the consumers. The natural apathy of people in general, means that they unwittingly settle for second best because that's what they are used to.

A newer entrant into such a market has the ability to harness this passive discontent, just as Lawrence did with the Arabs, by hitting the competition in the three places that you are able to and in the places that hurt them the most: quality, service and price. You can divide the competition by offering a better quality product, with a swifter, more personal service and a cheaper price. The most lethal tactic is to spark a price war, which is the last thing incumbent firms want. A price war hurts every firm except the protagonist. For the established players, large marketing budgets in spite of the costs, are more profitable than selling at lower prices. This is because non-price competition acts as an expensive barrier to entry for new smaller players. Therefore dividing the competition means taking the initiative on the fronts where you are able to compete and getting the established companies to compete with each other so that they really have to earn their money. The winners in all of this are of course the consumers and the shrewd protagonist who instigates and exploits the discord.

In 1942 the economist Joseph Schumpeter coined the term 'creative destruction'. He defined this as the process of transformation that accompanies radical innovation. In Schumpeter's vision of capitalism, innovative entry by entrepreneurs was the force that sustained long-term economic growth, even as it destroyed the value of established companies that enjoyed some degree of power. Throughout history giants have always come undone at the hands of smaller, nimbler and more innovative competitors and the Arab Revolt is no exception.

37. The Map Is Not the Territory

The Arab War was not a conventional struggle and could not be won with the lazy metaphors of text-book doctrine which were likewise failing the Europeans at this time.

> "How many zealots could we have? At present we had nearly fifty thousand: sufficient for the day. It seemed the assets in this element of war were ours. If we realized our raw materials and were apt with them, then climate, railway, desert, and technical weapons could also be attached to our interests. The Turks were stupid; the Germans behind them dogmatical. They would believe that rebellion was absolute like war, and deal with it on the analogy of war. Analogy in human things was fudge, anyhow; and war upon rebellion was messy and slow, like eating soup with a knife."

Eating soup with a knife is a good analogy but it is only an analogy. We must beware of mistaking analogous relationships with actual relationships. The Polish-American philosopher Alfred Korzybski encapsulated this understanding when he stated that 'The map is not the territory'.

People all too easily mix up the difference between reality and the internal representation of reality created by our senses — what we see, hear, smell, taste and touch. These senses are combined to create a mirror of reality — a map. But it is important to note that this is not reality itself.

When somebody says something is gospel true and indeed what a thousand people say is gospel true, is not necessarily true. Reality is an ever-changing point which exists only temporarily. Therefore as soon as someone declares something as absolutely infallible it inevitably becomes arguable or untrue from some perspective.

People will always tell you that you have to do a process in a certain way because that's the way it has always been done. Or people will earnestly insist that a certain market is saturated or a product or idea will not work. No matter how senior the naysayers may be, entrepreneurs have to possess enough independence and scepticism to think in the opposite direction to the common consensus — which is often just a lazy affirmation of what others have been told.

38. Practice Makes Perfection

The reality is that scientific understanding is not enough to win the war. There is a further 'biological' element which is beyond measurement but which holds a crucial role in the outcome of battle. It is in understanding and mastering this human element where generals make their reputations.

> "The 'felt' element in troops, not expressible in figures, had to be guessed at by the equivalent of Plato's δόξα [doksa — glory], and the greatest commander of men was he whose intuitions most nearly happened. Nine-tenths of tactics were certain enough to be teachable in schools; but the irrational tenth was like the kingfisher flashing across the pool, and in it lay the test of generals. It could be ensued only by instinct (sharpened by thought practising the stroke) until at the crisis it came naturally, a reflex. There had been men whose δόξα so nearly approached perfection that by its road they reached the certainty of ἐπιστήμη [epistimi — scientific knowledge]. The Greeks might have called such genius for command νόησις [noesis — intuitive knowledge]; had they bothered to rationalize revolt."

In *The Prince* Machiavelli illustrates Lawrence's understanding of how a general cultivates his instinct.

> 'Philopoemen, Prince of the Achaeans, among other praises which writers have bestowed on him, is commended because in time of peace he never had anything in his mind but the rules of war; and when he was in the country with friends, he often stopped and reasoned with them: "If the enemy should be upon that hill, and we should find ourselves here with our army, with whom would be the advantage? How should one best advance to meet him, keeping the ranks? If we should wish to retreat, how ought we to set about it? If they should retreat, how ought we to pursue?" And he would set forth to them, as he went, all the chances that could befall an army; he would listen to their opinion and state his, confirming it with reasons, so that by these continual discussions there could never arise, in time of war, any unexpected circumstances that he could not deal with.'

Fellow Italian, contemporary and probably the cleverest man in human history, Leonardo da Vinci, wrote that 'experience is the mother of wisdom'. The truth is that we only truly know something when we have practised it over and over. You can learn a lot of things from reading books, but that knowledge is no substitute for actually doing something. Thinkers down the ages stemming from Plato to Einstein have always stated that intuitive or instinctive understanding is a greater form of intelligence than declarative knowledge.

Reading books and listening to stories about business will only get you so far. Actually going out and working, and failing and succeeding with entrepreneurial zeal is what really counts towards learning. In this way you develop a type of subconscious and implicit ability to instinctively perceive and make the right choices.

39. Elevate the Individual over the Group

Lawrence gains a brilliant insight into providing the Arabs with a genuine advantage.

"My mind seesawed back to apply this to ourselves, and at once knew that it was not bounded by mankind, that it applied also to materials. In Turkey things were scarce and precious, men less esteemed than equipment. Our cue was to destroy, not the Turk's army, but his minerals. The death of a Turkish bridge or rail, machine or gun or charge of high explosive, was more profitable to us than the death of a Turk. In the Arab Army at the moment we were chary both of materials and of men. Governments saw men only in mass; but our men, being irregulars, were not formations, but individuals. An individual death, like a pebble dropped in water, might make but a brief hole; yet rings of sorrow widened out therefrom. We could not afford casualties."

This conception is shrewd and cunning — exactly the qualities needed by entrepreneurs. On the subject of human resources, the management guru Tom Peters once said that 'people are people — not personnel.' Armies (perhaps the only place where the word 'personnel' is still used) take away people's individuality and assign everyone a number as if they are robots incapable of thought, there to just do what they are told. Large companies do this too. They treat the staff as a payroll and a commodity. Many employees thus see the company as a faceless organisation and do whatever they can to avoid real work. They become wage slaves devoid of all creativity and love of the job. You may also get the situation that you see in China, where the labour pool is so large that companies will hire two people to do one job and managers don't delegate enough because they don't want their subordinates too see how easy their duties are. Too many people suffer from the disease of being obsessed with and limited by job titles so they never try new things or learn about other aspects of the business. Human beings are so much more than job titles. Each person is different and a mine of various knowledge and skills that can be tapped into for the good of the enterprise, regardless of credentials or titles.

Needless to say, the asymmetric entrepreneur needs to instil a culture of initiative, pride, and independence as well as break down departmental barriers among staff. The best working environment is a family meritocracy where ideas are encouraged and people at all levels are educated in the company ethos and genuinely rewarded for their efforts so that they feel a sense of ownership and credit in the success of the company, like players in a football team rather than a herd of sheep.

> 'If you find a job you love you will never work another day in your life.' ~ attributed to Confucius

40. Have an Edge in Just One Crucial Area

By putting flesh on the theory, he finds not just originality but a truly elegant form.

> "Materials were easier to replace. It was our obvious policy to be superior in some one tangible branch; gun-cotton or machine-guns or whatever could be made decisive. Orthodoxy had laid down the maxim, applied to men, of being superior at the critical point and moment of attack. We might be superior in equipment in one dominant moment or respect; and for both things and men we might give the doctrine a twisted negative side, for cheapness' sake, and be weaker than the enemy everywhere except in that one point or matter. The decision of what was critical would always be ours. Most wars were wars of contact, both forces striving into touch to avoid tactical surprise. Ours should be a war of detachment. We were to contain the enemy by the silent threat of a vast unknown desert, not disclosing ourselves till we attacked. The attack might be nominal, directed not against him, but against his stuff; so it would not seek either his strength or his weakness, but his most accessible material. In railway-cutting it would be usually an empty stretch of rail; and the more empty, the greater the tactical success. We might turn our average into a rule (not a law, since war was antinomian) and develop a habit of never engaging the enemy. This would chime with the numerical plea for never affording a target. Many Turks on our front had no chance all the war to fire on us, and we were never on the defensive except by accident and in error."

If you do one thing well and you know it better than anyone, make a virtue of it and promote it to the forefront of your operations. Make that aspect of your expertise a shining light which you can continually differentiate yourself with and outdo your competition. For Lawrence this superiority was in one piece of technology, the automatic rifle, combined with the innovative inverted strategy of the irregular army. For the entrepreneur it may be something similar like a special product line, the use of a particular machine, piece of software or an area of specialist expertise.

The term 'economic moat' was coined by the legendary investor Warren Buffett to describe the unassailable advantage a brand may have over its counterparts, such as a secret recipe, a patent, or sole access to a cheap supplier, which make it very difficult for any other company to simply copy the formula. It is a type of protectionism and barrier to entry that rests upon the uniqueness of a product, differentiating it from the commodified nature of products in perfect competition such as potatoes or coal. Steve Jobs is a fine example of somebody who created economic moats by developing revolutionary new technologies and keeping ahead of the industry by fiercely protecting their advantages and exclusivity with proprietary measures to prevent copying.

'If you don't have a competitive advantage, don't compete.' ~ Jack Welch

41. Pride Your Organisation on Intelligence

To make this a workable philosophy Lawrence realises that the Arabs need extra-special knowledge of the enemy and the territory.

"The corollary of such a rule was perfect 'intelligence', so that we could plan in certainty. The chief agent must be the general's head; and his understanding must be faultless, leaving no room for chance. Morale, if built on knowledge, was broken by ignorance. When we knew all about the enemy we should be comfortable. We must take more pains in the service of news than any regular staff."

Respect for intelligence and an enshrined culture of knowledge-sharing is how you really beat competition. Too often people in corporations are unaware of the motives and reasoning that the management work by. This is a very old fashioned style of management which serves to keep people in the dark so they don't get ambitious ideas above their station.

With a small amount of extra effort in communications, companies can educate even the lowest level workers as to the principles of the enterprise, the manifesto of the corporation — not some bland vacuous mission statement but a concrete and congruent philosophy which enables leadership roles to emerge at every echelon.

Knowledge is power and with the internet there is very little knowledge which is beyond the grasp of an individual. Education inspires and empowers people and this benefits the whole firm. A healthy company, therefore, should be a company of teachers who love to share knowledge, exchange opinions and guide people, regardless of their level or department. If everyone is a teacher, then that company cannot have a more responsible culture.

42. Learn from the Classics

With the algebraical and biological nature of the theory appearing to 'fit like a glove' Lawrence turns to the final pillar.

> "There remained the psychological element to build up into an apt shape. I went to Xenophon and stole, to name it, his word *Diathetics*, which had been the art of Cyrus before he struck."

Lawrence was the first person to write such a poetic and lucid military treatise since Xenophon, the ancient Greek warrior and scholar who was the personal tutor to Alexander the Great. Because he was such an erudite historian, Lawrence was able to delve back through history to find lessons of value, long forgotten by the modern world but applicable nonetheless.

Entrepreneurs, creatives and marketers likewise need to practice this because the one great constant that historians understand is that history repeats itself. History holds the door to a bottomless pit of concepts and inspiration which can be recycled and readapted. Look at these three quotes that exemplify this spirit.

> 'The past is certain, the future obscure.' ~ Thales

> 'A great value of antiquity lies in the fact that its writings are the only ones that modern men still read with exactness.' ~ Nietzsche

> 'Employ your time in improving yourself by other men's writings, so that you shall gain easily what others have laboured hard for.' ~ Socrates

43. Create a Unique Ethos and Propagate It in the Minds of All

From the final 'psychological' pillar to his theory comes a need to develop a suitable body of propaganda. this has the effect of moulding the crowd and bringing people on board emotionally.

> "It was more subtle than tactics, and better worth doing, because it dealt with uncontrollables, with subjects incapable of direct command. It considered the capacity for mood of our men, their complexities and mutability, and the cultivation of whatever in them promised to profit our intention. We had to arrange their minds in order of battle just as carefully and as formally as other officers would arrange their bodies. And not only our own men's minds, though naturally they came first. We must also arrange the minds of the enemy, so far as we could reach them; then those other minds of the nation supporting us behind the firing line, since more than half the battle passed there in the back; then the minds of the enemy nation waiting the verdict; and of the neutrals looking on; circle beyond circle."

Diathetic means a predisposition to certain illnesses in a person's body. In this context Lawrence uses the concept to mean planting seeds in people's minds, seeds to corrupt the enemy and develop their weaknesses. But it also means planting seeds of inspiration in the Arab army and the general populace, to make them believe in themselves and the cause. Lawrence takes the initiative from the Turks and keeps it. He humiliates them in their situations of backwardness, encumberedness and conventional dogma.

Cyrus the Great and Julius Caesar both used this method of exploiting weak dispositions in defeating their enemies. Originally Xenophon coined the concept from his study of Cyrus, and Caesar subsequently studied and emulated it.

In one famous battle with the Massagetae tribe, Cyrus heard that they were not familiar with the habit of drinking wine so he set up a fake camp near the enemy territory, stocked it with wine and left it guarded by the worst of his soldiers. The enemy overran the camp and duly became drunk so that when Cyrus swooped in with his best men he slaughtered them easily.

Caesar, when fighting the barbarian king Ariovistus, was frustrated by the enemy's refusal to attack. He then discovered from a captured prisoner that the Germans fought only when their gods deemed it favourable. On this occasion the heavens had shown it necessary to wait until the new moon. The next day Caesar promptly led out his army and attacked, leaving the Germans no other choice but to draw out their forces and be defeated on Roman terms.

It is interesting that Lawrence touches on the idea of concentric circles, because as members of a community and as protagonists in a market we are inherently connected to everyone else through waves of metaphysical energy. That is, the energy of emotions. We both give off and receive emotional energy, some of which is positive and some negative. Harnessing this is the business of leaders whether that be family, school, work, community, business or national leaders. Each group that you interact with represents a concentric circle. Recognising and managing your emotions and the emotions of others within these circles is the key to success and harmony in life. A leader unites his groups with positive language and encouragement and he divides his enemies with negative language and ideas.

44. Metaphysical Weapons are Greater than Physical Ones

The realisation that the Arab struggle is a modern war without the traditions and preconceptions of earlier times means that victory can be achieved on their own terms.

> "There were many humiliating material limits, but no moral impossibilities; so that the scope of our diathetical activities was unbounded. On it we should mainly depend for the means of victory on the Arab front: and the novelty of it was our advantage. The printing press, and each newly-discovered method of communication favoured the intellectual above the physical, civilization paying the mind always from the body's funds. We kindergarten soldiers were beginning our art of war in the atmosphere of the twentieth century, receiving our weapons without prejudice. To the regular officer, with the tradition of forty generations of service behind him, the antique arms were the most honoured. As we had seldom to concern ourselves with what our men did, but always with what they thought, the diathetic for us would be more than half the command. In Europe it was set a little aside, and entrusted to men outside the General Staff. In Asia the regular elements were so weak that irregulars could not let the metaphysical weapon rust unused."

The emotional role of a leader to inspire people is more important than intelligence or technical skills. Traditional intelligence is something that is fixed at birth — it is a physical trait wired into one's genes but as Benjamin Disraeli said, the greater power of emotional intelligence and intuition is cultivated through education and training.

Human beings are not rational and logical creatures, we are emotional beings and the person who can harness people's feelings will ultimately have more influence than the person who appeals to book-based logical practices, traditional processes and inherited techniques.

As the saying goes, the pen is mightier than the sword, and people's minds are more powerful than physical tools. Unlike the Turks,

Lawrence wisely places a higher value on the spiritual nature of lives than physical material and property.

Like Lawrence, we need to be ready to attack commoditisation of the market by tearing up the rule book. As we saw in Lesson 37, sometimes the best way forward is to reject the way people have traditionally used resources and done their jobs. We could all do well to remember these words from one of the world's greatest entrepreneurs.

'The first rule of business is that there are no rules.' ~ Richard Branson

45. Be Closer to Your Community than Your Competition

After eight days lying prostrate in a tent, Lawrence had conceptualised a new form of war that turned on its head all dominant military convention. On recovery he finalises his thoughts and prepares to put them into action.

> "It seemed to me proven that our rebellion had an unassailable base, guarded not only from attack, but from the fear of attack. It had a sophisticated alien enemy, disposed as an army of occupation in an area greater than could be dominated effectively from fortified posts. It had a friendly population, of which some two in the hundred were active, and the rest quietly sympathetic to the point of not betraying the movements of the minority. The active rebels had the virtues of secrecy and self-control, and the qualities of speed, endurance and independence of arteries of supply. They had technical equipment enough to paralyse the enemy's communications. A province would be won when we had taught the civilians in it to die for our ideal of freedom. The presence of the enemy was secondary. Final victory seemed certain, if the war lasted long enough for us to work it out."

In both thought and deed it is good to tap into what people genuinely understand, what they think they want and what they might not realise they want. That is authentic marketing and it's more engaging and trustworthy than mass market spam-like campaigns that don't connect with people's deeper desires and needs.

Community marketing is about building strong relationships with people at street level and not at the point of sale. It is about using new media to provide value and education not directly related to sales but related to the field in general. It is about not being desperate to sell a product and constantly repeating your message, but about being an active participant in a group. A human being and an expert, who is contactable, can answer questions and give opinions whether online or off. If you do that then the sales will come in a tertiary, more lucrative and permanent way.

46. Don't Openly Attack Competition

On their new mission to hit the railway the rebels spend the day in full view of the enemy garrison to the annoyance and bemusement of the Turks. At night the men go back to the track and start wreaking havoc.

> "Then, to explain ourselves plausibly to the enemy, we began blowing up things to the north of the mine. We found a little four-arch bridge and put it into the air. Afterwards we turned to rails and cut about two hundred: and while the men were laying and lighting charges I taught Mohammed to climb a splintery pole; together we cut the wires, and with their purchase dragged down other poles. All was done at speed, for we feared lest Turks come after us: and when our explosive work was finished we ran back like hares to our camels, mounted them, and trotted without interruption down the windy valley once more to the plain of Hamdh."

As we saw in Lesson 28, Lawrence used subtle sabotage; hitting the railway just enough to cripple the Turks while not forcing retreat or an offensive from them. Lawrence had figured out that making the maintenance of the Turkish garrison at Medina just a shade less difficult than its evacuation, would serve the interests of the British and Arabs alike.

It is costly and dangerous to attack your competition outright. Subtlety means finding the balance between proximity and avoidance. You can infuriate your opponents by sticking close to them but always implying why your service or product is better.

Attacking people directly says more about you than it does about them and it can backfire if they decide to go after you. Sophisticated marketing is about taking a third way. It means not even mentioning the competition but appropriately evangelising about how different and new your own product or service is. This leaves people to figure out the difference and the reality for themselves, which is always a superior, more convincing form of motivation.

47. Adopt the Pareto Rule

At breakfast the next day after laying the mine, the raiders hear two huge explosions coming from the railway in the distance.

> "Before bread was baked the scouts arrived, to tell us that at dawn the Turks had been busy round our damages; and a little later a locomotive with trucks of rails, and a crowded labour gang on top, had come up from Hedia, and had exploded the mine fore and aft of its wheels. This was everything we had hoped, and we rode back to Abdullah's camp on a morning of perfect springtime, in a singing company. We had proved that a well-laid mine would fire; and that a well-laid mine was difficult even for its maker to discover. These points were of importance; for Newcombe, Garland and Hornby were now out upon the railway, harrying it: and mines were the best weapon yet discovered to make the regular working of their trains costly and uncertain for our Turkish enemy."

Pareto efficiency is a very general rule of thumb that is used throughout industry. With it you build on successes and drop the things that don't work; channelling that time, money or effort into the things which bring results. Thereby over time, resources naturally become allocated to where they work best. Pareto efficiency ties with the concept of requisite variety discussed in Chapter 11 which states that if you are not getting the results you desire, you have to change something and keep changing it until you get the result you're looking for. Good marketers seek out the avenues that work best and play on them, getting the maximum returns possible.

Winston Churchill had the headache of trying to win the North African Campaign against Rommel in World War II but was unable to find competent commanders. He had to remove general after general until he found Montgomery, who rebuilt morale, turned the fighting around and took the Allies on to victory. Churchill didn't give up, he just made personnel changes until it he eventually got the right formula.

48. Don't Rely on Promises

Lawrence goes on to describe the court, behaviour and character of Prince Abdullah in contrast to his younger brother, Faisal.

> "He affected to have no care for the Hejaz situation, regarding the autonomy of the Arabs as assured by the promises of Great Britain to his father, and leaning at ease against this prop. I longed to tell him that the half-witted old man had obtained from us no concrete or unqualified undertaking of any sort, and that their ship might founder on the bar of his political stupidity; but that would have been to give away my English masters, and the mental tug of war between honesty and loyalty, after swaying a while, settled again expediently into deadlock."

Lawrence has a very cynical attitude which in this instance is healthy because you cannot rely on the assistance of others in lieu of your own preparations. The world is not perfect but people still indulge in wishful thinking, which is a disease of salesmanship, business deals, partnerships and project forecasting.

Things get promised in the optimism of the moment but circumstances can and do change. If you have banked on cash or equipment or assistance from people, it's better to keep expectations low to avoid disappointment and difficulties. Assistance is nice when you get it but ultimately we have to rely on our own forces not those of others.

49. Don't View Cultures in Binary Opposition

Riding back to Wajh, Lawrence gives another of his cultural sketches illustrating the activities and personalities of his Bedouin comrades. In particular he describes how they live a completely different existence to civilised city-dwellers.

> "If they suspected that we wanted to drive them either they were mulish or they went away. If we comprehended them, and gave time and trouble to make things tempting to them, then they would go to great pains for our pleasure. Whether the results achieved were worth the effort, no man could tell. Englishmen, accustomed to greater returns, would not, and, indeed, could not, have spent the time, thought and tact lavished every day by sheikhs and emirs for such meagre ends. Arab processes were clear, Arab minds moved logically as our own, with nothing radically incomprehensible or different, except the premiss: there was no excuse or reason, except our laziness and ignorance, whereby we could call them inscrutable or Oriental, or leave them misunderstood.
>
> They would follow us, if we endured with them, and played the game according to their rules. The pity was, that we often began to do so, and broke down with exasperation and threw them over, blaming them for what was a fault in our own selves. Such strictures like a general's complaint of bad troops, were in reality a confession of our faulty foresight, often made falsely out of mock modesty to show that, though mistaken, we had at least the wit to know our fault."

It is all too easy to view new cultures with suspicion, distrust and perhaps look down on them but this is actually an irrational approach. The psychological phenomenon of projection is where we tend to view the shortcomings in our own culture as magnified in the cultures of others. In fact, human societies are far more homogeneous than people give them credit for.

It serves to be a cultural relativist in a modern globalised world and that means understanding that there are no superior or inferior cultures. It's too easy to generalise whole populations as stupid or primitive and 'not like us'. The more rigorous and sensitive person prefers not to judge but to dig deeper and try to understand on a person by person basis. Fools assume they are *prima facie* correct and seek to cast aspersions, wise men assume they may be mistaken and seek to understand.

50. Take the Time to Crystallise Your Philosophy

Back at Wajh, the leadership settles into a mood of confidence and cohesiveness. Lawrence decides to explain his new found ideas to Faisal and Joyce, his commanding officers, and dissuade them from the original plan of taking Medina.

> "All this programme was what I had believed necessary for the further progress of the Arab Revolt when we took Wejh. I had planned and arranged some of it myself. But now, since that happy fever and dysentery in Abdulla's camp had given me leisure to meditate upon the strategy and tactics of irregular war, it seemed that not merely the details but the essence of this plan were wrong. It therefore became my business to explain my changed ideas, and if possible to persuade my chiefs to follow me into the new theory.
>
> So I began with three propositions. Firstly, that irregulars would not attack places, and so remained incapable of forcing a decision. Secondly, that they were as unable to defend a line or point as they were to attack it. Thirdly, that their virtue lay in depth, not in face."

Lawrence is continually questioning his assumptions and he gives much of his time to the raw task of thinking. Complex ideas become simpler and more elegant through long periods of deep thought.

> 'Thinking is the hardest work there is, which is probably the reason why so few engage in it.' ~ Henry Ford

If you can take the time to be one of the few, then you can steal a march on competitors, innovate new ideas and lead the field. The leader of an organisation needs to think more than anyone else. This is where the real gold comes from. Everything else can be essentially delegated from the top but the true innovation is found in deep thought. The point is that leaders are needed at every level of an organisation and therefore those who take the time to consider the business are the ones who go the furthest.

We have already noted that successful people spend a good period of each day away from distractions — where they can crystallise their thoughts in isolation. Creativity cannot occur unless you have long sessions without distraction in which to play and come to terms with the project you are working on.

The trick sometimes is to try to think of nothing. The irony is that most people feel they are wasting time by sitting in silence, not 'producing' anything. That, however, is a short sighted way to view work and is precisely what Henry Ford is referring to.

51. Use Hardship as a Rite of Passage

Lawrence is convinced that the Arabs must realign their strategy to match the Bedouins' and the territory's inherent strengths.

> The Arab war was geographical, and the Turkish Army an accident. Our aim was to seek the enemy's weakest material link and bear only on that till time made their whole length fail. Our largest resources, the Beduin on whom our war must be built, were unused to formal operations, but had assets of mobility, toughness, self-assurance, knowledge of the country, intelligent courage. With them dispersal was strength. Consequently we must extend our front to its maximum, to impose on the Turks the longest possible passive defence, since that was, materially, their most costly form of war.
>
> Our duty was to attain our end with the greatest economy of life, since life was more precious to us than money or time. If we were patient and superhuman-skilled, we could follow the direction of Saxe and reach victory without battle, by pressing our advantages mathematical and psychological. Fortunately our physical weakness was not such as to demand this. We were richer than the Turks in transport, machine-guns, cars, high explosive. We could develop a highly mobile, highly equipped striking force of the smallest size, and use it successively at distributed points of the Turkish line, to make them strengthen their posts beyond the defensive minimum of twenty men. This would be a short cut to success.

Hardship is often a pre-requisite for success. Employees who have had it easy all their lives will with great difficulty get used to striving for goals, pushing comfort zones, and putting the business before themselves. But people who have experienced hardship know how to surmount obstacles, have survived crises and have the hunger and drive to move forward with the goal in sight. Good managers will create obstacles if none exist, to provide a foil on which to rise higher and gain insights. As we saw in Lesson 30, doing things the hard way is often the best way and successful people don't shy away from tough situations and responsibilities.

An entrepreneur should seek to develop a team who are not necessarily experienced but possess all the adjectives of Lawrence's Bedouins: a band of highly independent individuals who can operate in a dispersed fashion with initiative and courage. Economy of effort is the key to organisations working under limited resources and constraints. Teams who know their strengths and weaknesses and are educated to work within them — not simply adhering to the usual rules of the game, are the teams who become the strongest. Money and materials that come later then become a big plus that get used to the maximum rather than an easily available necessity that is taken for granted.

52. Use Your Competitor's Strength Against Him

This new way of fighting was far easier and more sensible than trying to get the Turks to evacuate and letting them subsequently regroup in a better place.

> "We must not take Medina. The Turk was harmless there. In prison in Egypt he would cost us food and guards. We wanted him to stay at Medina, and every other distant place, in the largest numbers. Our ideal was to keep his railway just working, but only just, with the maximum of loss and discomfort. The factor of food would confine him to the railways, but he was welcome to the Hejaz Railway, and the Trans-Jordan railway, and the Palestine and Syrian railways for the duration of the war, so long as he gave us the other nine hundred and ninety-nine thousandths of the Arab world. If he tended to evacuate too soon, as a step to concentrating in the small area which his numbers could dominate effectually, then we should have to restore his confidence by reducing our enterprises against him. His stupidity would be our ally, for he would like to hold, or to think he held, as much of his old provinces as possible. This pride in his imperial heritage would keep him in his present absurd position--all flanks and no front."

Pragmatic entrepreneurs attack with the line of least resistance when battling in the market by accepting the existence of competitors as being harmless where they lie. Let competitors keep the illusion that they are holding territory when in fact they are leaking money with expensive overheads and bloated budgets, deluded in the belief that market share is more important than profitability; that consolidation is pre-eminent to strategic innovation; that today is more important than tomorrow.

If we revisit the principle that the map is not the territory, we could say in this context it means that new firms can, as a rule, allow established firms' pride and hubris to cloud their view of reality. The situation on the ground is the last thing many firms notice because as Caesar said,

> 'Men in general are quick to believe that which they wish to be true.'

Chapter V

Lessons 53 — 63

Strategies for Competing

Extending to Aqaba — Précis

By mid-spring the campaign was going well and the town of Aqaba was the next target. Lawrence begins the march with a band of men including the famed warlord Auda. This nomad army, numbering around fifty men, undertake an epic journey through the desert from west to east in which Lawrence describes the eerie landscape in beautiful lucid detail. Eventually the men reach a camp and are treated to great hospitality while they plot the assault on the key coastal town to link up with the British Navy. The campaign gathers momentum as the force swells tenfold and the men terrorise and foil the miserable and machinelike Turks, finally forcing their surrender at Aqaba without loss.

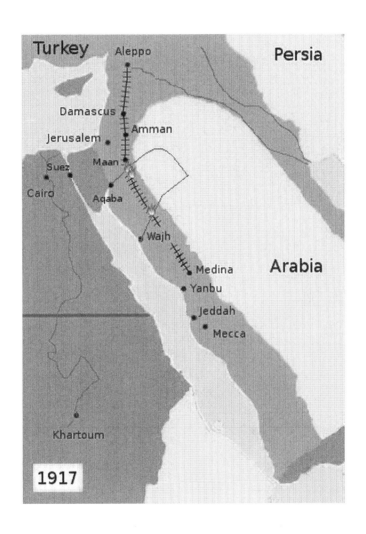

"*The port of Akaba was naturally so strong that it could be taken only by surprise from inland: but the opportune adherence to Feisal of Auda Abu Tayi made us hope to enrol enough tribesmen in the eastern desert for such a descent upon the coast.*

Nasir, Auda, and I set off together on the long ride. Hitherto Feisal had been the public leader: but his remaining in Sejh threw the ungrateful load of this northern expedition upon myself. I accepted it and its dishonest implication as our only means of victory. We tricked the Turks and entered Akaba with good fortune."

Lessons 53 — 63

Strategies for Competing

53. Set the Example

Riding through the desert with a small Arab force, they spot a group of strangers from afar. After a while they recognise the leader as Hornby, the railway saboteur and partner in crime of Newcombe. These two men were known throughout the Hejaz for their skills and accomplishments in smashing the railway.

> "Arabs told me Newcombe would not sleep except head on rails, and that Hornby would worry the metals with his teeth when gun-cotton failed. These were legends, but behind them lay a sense of their joint insatiate savagery in destroying till there was no more to destroy. Four Turkish labour battalions they kept busy, patching culverts, relaying sleepers, jointing new rails; and gun-cotton had to come in increasing tons to Wejh to meet their appetites. They were wonderful, but their too-great excellence discouraged our feeble teams, making them ashamed to exhibit their inferior talent: so Newcombe and Hornby remained as individualists, barren of the seven-fold fruits of imitation."

The two men that Lawrence describes set the example with an inhuman capacity for action and endurance. As we saw in Lessons 7 and 29, leaders must keep people in awe of themselves. They don't expect others to work harder than they do and they pride themselves on generating ideas. Unlike Newcombe and Hornby though, they must also strive to make themselves accessible, teach others their techniques and make themselves progressively unnecessary.

> 'If one person can do something, anyone else can learn to do it.' ~ Bandler & Grinder

Broadly speaking, there are two ways to lead: one by delegation, in other words, telling people what to do. The other by example: demonstrating what to do. The best leaders do both but, like Caesar, favour the latter because although it takes more courage, it inspires people more to see their leader in action. A good leader should be ready to say: watch me and emulate me.

In leading by delegation, intelligence is not a pre-requisite. Intelligence can be possessed by the people you delegate to. But in the second instance, a leader must have the zeal and noesis honed through practice and discipline to go into action himself, just as the two British saboteurs do.

'Nothing makes a prince so much esteemed as great enterprises and setting a fine example.' ~ Machiavelli

54. Don't Give Up on Lost Causes

On the next day's march Lawrence discovers that one of the travellers in the party, the much-disliked Syrian peasant, Gasim, is missing. The thick-skinned Arabs do not care to search for the lost man but Lawrence decides to turn back.

"I looked weakly at my trudging men, and wondered for a moment if I could change with one, sending him back on my camel to the rescue. My shirking the duty would be understood, because I was a foreigner: but that was precisely the plea I did not dare set up, while I yet presumed to help these Arabs in their own revolt. It was hard, anyway, for a stranger to influence another people's national movement, and doubly hard for a Christian and a sedentary person to sway Moslem nomads. I should make it impossible for myself if I claimed, simultaneously, the privileges of both societies.

So, without saying anything, I turned my unwilling camel round, and forced her, grunting and moaning for her camel friends, back past the long line of men, and past the baggage into the emptiness behind. My temper was very unheroic, for I was furious with my other servants, with my own play-acting as a Beduin, and most of all with Gasim, a gap-toothed, grumbling fellow, skrimshank in all our marches, bad-tempered, suspicious, brutal, a man whose engagement I regretted, and of whom I had promised to rid myself as soon as we reached a discharging-place. It seemed absurd that I should peril my weight in the Arab adventure for a single worthless man.

[...]

I had ridden about an hour and a half, easily, for the following breeze had let me wipe the crust from my red eyes and look forward almost without pain: when I saw a figure, or large bush, or at least something black ahead of me. The shifting mirage disguised height or distance; but this thing seemed moving, a little east of our course. On chance I turned my camel's head that way, and in a few minutes saw that it was Gasim. When I called he stood confusedly; I rode up and saw that he was nearly blinded and silly, standing there with his arms held out to me, and his black mouth gaping open. The Ageyl had put our last water in my skin, and this he spilled madly over his face and breast, in haste to drink. He stopped babbling, and began to wail out his sorrows. I sat him, pillion, on the camel's rump; then stirred her up and mounted.

[...]

Not four miles had passed when again I saw a black bubble, lunging and swaying in the mirage ahead. It split into three, and swelled. I wondered if they were enemy. A minute later the haze unrolled with the disconcerting suddenness of illusion; and it was Auda with two of Nasir's men come back to look for me. I yelled jests and scoffs at them for abandoning a friend in the desert. Auda pulled his beard and grumbled that had he been present I would never have gone back. Gasim was transferred with insults to a better rider's saddlepad, and we ambled forward together."

Lawrence earns himself a lot of kudos for doing this. Yet again he doesn't take the easy option that everyone is all too happy to absolve themselves with. In work similarly, commitment and persistence are the keys to success. By putting yourself on the radar and volunteering for the things that others ignore, you can prove yourself and get noticed and ultimately do what is right for the company.

The old saying goes that a chain is only as strong as its weakest link and that means that being a team player and having a strong team requires looking after the strugglers where necessary, developing people and finding the best in them and not just giving up on things. That is how winning teams emerge.

55. Be Assertive and Ready for Action

After a five-day trek through searing heat and battering sandstorms in a vast foreboding part of the desert known as Al Houl, meaning 'The Terror', they settle for the night in a small group of hills nearby a well.

"The mass did not arrive for an hour or more, when the wind had altogether died away, and the evening, calm and black and full of stars, had come down on us. Auda set a watch through the night, for this district was in the line of raiding parties, and in the hours of darkness there were no friends in Arabia.

[later]

Hardly, however, had our messenger ridden off when one of the Howeitat saw riders hiding in the scrub to the northward of us.

Instantly they called to arms. Mohammed el Dheilan, first into the saddle, with other Toweiha galloped out against the supposed enemy; Nasir and I mustered the Ageyl (whose virtue lay not in fighting Beduin-fashion with Beduins) and placed them in sets about the dunes so as reasonably to defend the baggage. However, the enemy got off. Mohammed returned after half an hour to say that he had not made relentless pursuit for pity of the condition of his camel. He had seen only three tracks and supposed that the men had been scouts of a Shammar raiding party in the neighbourhood, Arfaja being commonly infested by them."

Lawrence's men are not passive in their approach to others. In the desert everyone is a potential friend or foe and you need to be constantly prepared for both. The scarcity of resources forces men to band together and attack on a whim while it forces others to hold fast to what they have.

Always be ready to attack or defend. Passivity is more dangerous than fight because passivity is weak, lazy and it breaks the group bond. Aggression is also bad for the same reason but Lawrence's men do not pursue with complete aggression; they know the line to tread, beyond which a viable 'lost cause' becomes a dangerous and wasteful folly.

Rather, they give a measured response and do just enough to chase away the enemy.

In staff relations and in dealings with others, assertiveness means doing the right thing for both yourself and the company. Assertiveness is the positive balance between aggression and passivity which keeps a community and organisation strong.

56. Think Big

As the desert march gathers force Lawrence has to quickly and with good reason counteract the urge of Nesib, the intemperate Syrian commander. Lawrence tries to persuade him that rather than make a rash strike for Damascus they should pursue the original plan of capturing Aqaba on the Red Sea coast.

"The Arabs needed Akaba: firstly, to extend their front, which was their tactical principle; and, secondly, to link up with the British. If they took it the act gave them Sinai, and made positive junction between them and Sir Archibald Murray. Thus having become really useful, they would obtain material help. The human frailty of Murray's Staff was such that nothing but physical contact with our success could persuade them of our importance. Murray was friendly: but if we became his right wing he would equip us properly, almost without the asking. Accordingly, for the Arabs, Akaba spelt plenty in food, money, guns, advisers. I wanted contact with the British; to act as the right wing of the Allies in the conquest of Palestine and Syria; and to assert the Arabic-speaking peoples' desire or desert of freedom and self-government. In my view, if the revolt did not reach the main battlefield against Turkey it would have to confess failure, and remain a side-show of a side-show. I had preached to Feisal, from our first meeting, that freedom was taken, not given."

It is true that freedom is taken and not given. In business and in life success is won by those who work for it and fight for it every inch of the way. It is too easy to complain, make excuses and not do enough when opportunity or difficulty presents itself. Unfortunately there are far too many people who just expect everything to be handed to them on a plate.

In the real world of business, nothing is guaranteed and leaders need to do everything in their power to create their own reality. In this way if the finger of blame must be pointed, they can rest assured, knowing that failure was due to factors truly outside of their control. The people who win are the people who don't take shortcuts. Instead they do things the right way, dotting the i's and crossing the t's to personally ensure success.

'You must be the change you wish to see in the world.' ~ Gandhi

57. Never Interrupt an Enemy When He Is Making a Mistake

Lawrence uses all his common sense and guile to scotch Nesib's pipedream while dispossessing him of his gold by partially agreeing to support the folly.

"Both Nasir and Auda fortunately answered to my whispers; and, after recriminations, Nesib left us, and rode with Zeki to the Druse Mountain, there to do the preliminary work necessary to the launching of his great Damascus scheme. I knew his incapacity to create; but it was not in my mind to permit even a half-baked rising there, to spoil our future material. So I was careful to draw his teeth before he started, by taking from him most of the money Feisal had shared out to him. The fool made this easy for me, as he knew he had not enough for all he wanted; and, measuring the morality of England by his own pettiness, came to me for the promise of more if he raised a Syrian movement independent of Feisal, under his own leadership. I had no fear of so untoward a miracle; and, instead of calling him rat, gave my ready promise for future help, if he would for the present give me his balance, to get us to Akaba, where I would make funds available for the general need. He yielded to my condition with a bad grace; and Nasir was delighted to get two bags of money unexpectedly."

Lawrence takes a no-lose position and plays along with Nesib's scheme because he knows it is an unrealistic and flawed aim at this point in the campaign. He also takes the opportunity to strip him of his resources under the guise of assistance, neutralising the danger and playing him like the fool that he is.

In the context of negotiations, very often the other party may have unreasonable expectations of what you can deliver or for what price you can offer. In such a situation you can delay their contrivances by agreeing, but only on certain conditions. Then you make the conditions stacked in your favour that you protect yourself from being steamrollered into agreeing to something you didn't wish to.

58. Put People off the Scent

After finding the wells at Bair damaged by the Turks but not beyond repair, the men resolve to stay there, gather the support of the tribes in the region and suddenly attack the town of Abu al Lasan to the north near the railway.

> "Crux of our plan was the attack on Aba el Lissan, lest the force in Maan have time to sally out, relieve it, and drive us off the head of Shtar. If, as at present, they were only a battalion, they would hardly dare move; and should they let it fall while waiting for reinforcements to arrive, Akaba would surrender to us, and we should be based on the sea and have the advantageous gorge of Itm between us and the enemy. So our insurance for success was to keep Maan careless and weak, not suspecting our malevolent presence in the neighbourhood."

Lawrence recognised the strategic value of Aqaba being located on the coast, while the Turks ignored it because it was not near the railway. Lawrence used a feint to keep them away from it. As much as you need to enlighten your own people in a company, you also need to keep your opponents, competitors and sometimes your opposition in negotiations, equally in the dark and misdirected as to your game plan.

As Lawrence does continually in this chapter, you must confuse your opposite number by dropping misleading hints to make him divide his resources to your advantage. If your opponent applies pressure, then divert his attention to give yourself time to regain composure and get what it is you really want.

Formlessness is the key to not letting people read your motives. In any type of negotiations, you can't let people know what you really want from the outset. You need to guard your true intentions while using your intuition to feel what they want. Once you know that, you have leverage over them.

> 'Make a sound in the east, then strike in the west.' ~ Chinese proverb, *The Thirty-Six Stratagems*

59. Don't Despise Your Enemy

The Arabs knew that their operation was not a secret. There was no way of keeping their movements and their final destination from the Turks so they had to increase their use of deceptions.

> "However, there was no measuring the stupidity of the Turkish Army; a point which helped us now and again, and harmed us constantly, for we could not avoid despising them for it (Arabs being a race gifted with uncommon quickness of mind, and overvaluing it) and an army suffered when unable to yield honour to the enemy. For the moment the stupidity might be made use of; and so we had undertaken a prolonged campaign of deception, to convince them that our objective lay nearer to Damascus."

Despising your opponent is an emotional stance and it constitutes irrational thinking. It is preferable to see them for what they are rather than what we believe or wish them to be. It's hard to have respect for your opponents but it is a sign of maturity and rationality. The less you see people through an emotional lens, the more you can understand them and learn from them.

A classic example is Google's underestimation of Facebook. Google had been the dominant player for nearly a decade and its name is almost synonymous with the internet but they never predicted how a website could come along and offer something more enticing in the form of an internal economy of information based on social relationships and chat. They lost out on a hugely lucrative market because they were caught napping and didn't respect the opposition.

It is arrogant and egotistical to over-value your winning abilities, no matter how superior you may be. Although confidence is a great thing in business, once this steps over the line into hubristic pride then the potential for a fall is large. Although your opponent may be weak and foolish, observe them scientifically and keep your feet on the ground with constant reality checks.

60. Intuition Is a Better Judge than the Mind

While harrying out the railway they come across a Turkish station in possession of a flock of sheep. The hungry Arabs cannot resist taking the post and relieving it of its food supply.

> "Near the height of plundering came a pause and panic. The Arabs were such accustomed scouts that almost they felt danger before it came, sense taking precautions before mind was persuaded."

Successful, emotionally intelligent and experienced people listen to their intuition. It takes practice but your gut instinct is often a better judge of a situation than other people's opinions or what the mind perceives as ought to be.

Intuition can be described as a sixth sense but one which can be cultivated and one which allows us to read more into situations and communications than may appear at first sight. Asian people tend to use their intuition more than westerners because westerners are generally a bit more matter of fact in perceiving interpersonal relationships. Generally in interactions Asian people will try to imagine what the other party is thinking and feeling. They will make more of an effort to place themselves in the other person's shoes and see things from their perspective. In salesmanship, marketing and any form of negotiation, if you can tell what the other person wants, it means you have a certain degree of power over them.

Westerners on the other hand are slightly more open minded as to their relationship with their environment and what is possible to do in the future to change it, whereas Asians can be more accepting of environmental circumstances and constraints.

Both types of intuitive skills require the ability to visualise clearly. In a modern globalised context, many Asian people have to throw off the shackles of outmoded Confucianist teachings and attitudes towards authority if they wish to succeed. That means being more assertive in terms of their relationships with others and the future. Westerners equally have to learn to be less aggressive and more receptive in pursuit of their goals. If people can do this, they can be better negotiators and business people both at home and abroad and the world can be a more integrated and productive place.

'The only real valuable thing is intuition.' ~ Einstein

61. Let Hubris Reign in Your Opponent

After rebuilding a well at Jefer that the Turks tried to destroy, they send out a raiding party to attack another enemy post and secure the road to Aqaba.

> "We sat in Jefer meanwhile, waiting to hear the fortune of the attack. On its success or failure would depend the direction of our next march. The halt was not unpleasant, for our position had its comic side. We were within sight of Maan, during those minutes of the day in which the mirage did not make eyes and glasses useless; and yet we strolled about admiring our new well-lip in complete security, because the Turkish garrison believed water impossible here or at Bair, and were hugging the pleasant idea that we were now desperately engaged with their cavalry in Sirhan."

This is another example of the map-territory dissonance and wishful thinking discussed in the last chapter. Just because your competitors or opponents believe themselves to be in a strong position does not mean that they are so. Emotionally intelligent people don't step over the intuitive line and assume everything to be fact. They continually question their assumptions and never take things for granted.

The Turks are complacent like this because they are isolated. Isolation is the easiest way to lose touch with reality and with customers. When business leaders start taking decisions on their own without conferring and getting opinions from others, the potential for error is magnified. A trait of good leadership is to use the people you know as a sounding board for your ideas. Two heads are better than one, and ten heads are better than two heads.

Leaders ideally should be continually questioning the people closest to them to gain a greater perspective on the situation. Regardless of whether people's opinions are right or wrong, they want raw quantity to begin with. The true quality ideas can be sorted out only when you have a large enough sample.

62. Hold Firm on Your Strategy

After their successful raid on Abu al Lasan, Lawrence interrogates one of the prisoners and finds that the Turkish base at Ma'an is weakly defended.

> "This meant we could take it easily, and the Howeitat clamoured to be led there, lured by the dream of unmeasured loot, though what we had taken here was a rich prize. However, Nasir, and afterwards Auda, helped me stay them. We had no supports, no regulars, no guns, no base nearer than Wejh, no communications, no money even, for our gold was exhausted, and we were issuing our own notes, promises to pay 'when Akaba is taken', for daily expenses. Besides, a strategic scheme was not changed to follow up a tactical success. We must push to the coast, and re-open sea-contact with Suez."

The core definition of emotional intelligence is being able to put off present benefit in favour of future gain. To be a leader emotional intelligence is more important than anything else. In this instance, Lawrence's refusal to pander to the men's wishes was justified by his core strategy. Through the campaign Lawrence was educating the tribesmen by instilling in them a more emotionally intelligent spirit. The leaders of the Arab Revolt were pushing a new order of nationalism and political struggle which the Arabs had not considered before. They had always cared about their tribe and gone to war for wealth and parochial reasons.

Leaders sometimes have to go against the opinions of the many. Their job is to inspire greater ideals in their people. They raise up employees and consumers from small minded goals to a new paradigm; a new way of thinking; a new strategy and horizon. An intangible horizon of beliefs and ideals befits a more confident community — it represents a more ambitious crusade. No man is an island and we need the help of others to achieve anything of importance in life. Leaders though, have the vision and foresight to be stubborn when their central convictions and principles are called on or questioned. They are aware of the balance of when to listen and when to go beyond the immediately popular choice.

63. Strike From the Least Expected Place

After the victory the swollen Arab army trundles westward through the hills and valleys towards the Aqaba and the coast.

> "The narrows of Wadi Itm increased in intricate ruggedness as we penetrated deeper. Below Kethira we found Turkish post after Turkish post, empty. Their men had been drawn in to Khadra, the entrenched position (at the mouth of Itm), which covered Akaba so well against a landing from the sea. Unfortunately for them the enemy had never imagined attack from the interior, and of all their great works not one trench or post faced inland. Our advance from so new a direction threw them into panic."

The element of surprise was crucial for taking Aqaba and to the success of the whole campaign. In negotiations, product development, launches and marketing, the key to winning is keeping your cards close to your chest and then to strike when and where people least expect it.

Good marketing is about thinking differently and being different from everyone else. When you can do this, you can make other people think. It's about coming out of left field and offering or saying something unique that people aren't expecting. When you can do this, people sit up and take note. Good marketing resonates with peoples inner feelings and creates excitement because it's new.

One failsafe way of attracting attention is through controversy. Most of us think that being controversial is dangerous, but the most interesting people love to be controversial. And people love them because of it. The reason they can get away with extreme or different opinions is because they employ the five factors of rhetoric that have been around since Roman times. These are: facts, reason, logic, humour and politeness. If you make your advertising copy controversial and you employ the five factors, then you can surprise people and get their following. Using the shock factor means that you can and should advertise less but the advertising you do must be better than everyone around you in the marketplace.

Chapter VI

Lessons 64 — 78

Interpersonal Skills

Marking Time — Précis

Having captured Aqaba they set about securing it while the looming problem of a lack of food for the hugely swollen numbers of soldiers, prisoners and civilians needs to be addressed. Lawrence immediately undertakes another arduous journey, this time to Suez on a weak camel to request a supply ship and to report to his superiors in Cairo. Following this he flies to Jeddah to meet the King, finalise the plans and prevent possible treacherous overtures to the enemy by Auda. Having attended to these political matters Lawrence returns to Cairo by boat for a spell of respite.

The war was now entering a new phase. In Lawrence's words, at Wajh it was won and at Aqaba it was ended, and now the British were fully on board, the new challenge was to free Syria — a diverse and disjointed territory which includes the modern states of Israel, Palestine and Jordan. Lawrence goes on to describe in his great opinionated and cutting style the many ethnic and religious interweavings of this complex and ancient region. He also elucidates his revolutionary military philosophy and the logistics of fighting an 'articulated war' with highly independent irregular guerrillas.

Finally the Turkish Army shores up its position and begins to march out with the goal of retaking Aqaba. However, the Arabs harry them and make their lives difficult. Meanwhile Lawrence and a small gang of men including two British sergeants, journey out into the desert to blow up a train and raid an enemy garrison. Emboldened by the success of this strike, the Arabs resolve to increase their mining of trains to further weaken the Turks.

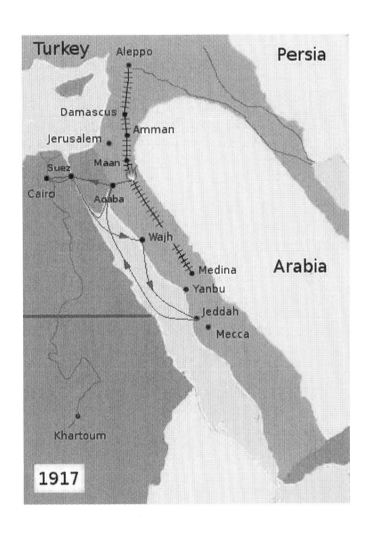

"*Our capture of Akaba closed the Hejaz war, and gave us the task of helping the British invade Syria. The Arabs working from Akaba became virtual right wing of Allenby's army in Sinai.*

To mark the changed relation Feisal, with his army, was transferred to Allenby's command. Allenby now became responsible for his operations and equipment. Meanwhile we organized the Akaba area as an unassailable base, from which to hinder the Hejaz railway."\

Lessons 64 — 78

Interpersonal Skills

64. Encourage Self-Sufficient Independent Units

Having captured Aqaba a post-victory lull sets in around the camp and while the alarming problem of hunger becomes evident, the leaders begin planning their next moves.

> "In the evening, our first reaction against success having passed off, we began to think how we should keep Akaba, having gained it. We settled that Auda should return to Guweira. He would there be covered by the descent of Shtar, and the Guweira sands. In fact, as safe as need be. But we would make him safer yet, in excess of precaution. We would put an outpost twenty miles to his north, in the impregnable rock-ruins of Nabathean Petra, and link them to him by a post at Delagha. Auda should also send men to Batra so that his Howeitat lie in a semicircle of four positions round the edge of the Maan highlands, covering every way towards Akaba.
>
> These four positions existed independently. The enemy had swallowed Goltz' impertinent generalities about the interdependence of strong-posts. We looked to their delivering a spirited drive against one, and sitting afterwards in it dazed for an uncomfortable month, unable to advance for the threat of the remaining three, scratching their heads and wondering why the others did not fall."

General Goltz was a German commander during World War I and the impertinent generalities that Lawrence refers to translate into a lazy and over-reliant way of viewing organisational interdependence.

It is important to instil a culture of self sufficiency and independence among branches so they are not constantly relying on Head Office or other branches for direction and resources. Individual branches must stand on their own two feet commercially, financially and managerially so that if a crisis does occur it can be dealt with locally causing minimal trouble.

The key to being able to do this is ensuring everyone is reading on the same page regarding a strong and common unifying goal and company manifesto. Staff at all levels must be enfranchised into the organisational ethos so that most issues do not have to be a matter of debate, confusion and deferral to superiors. The answers and policies are already well established, commonplace and even intuitive in the minds of employees. This is a very similar model to Richard Branson's Virgin group of companies. Virgin have a clear and celebrated organisational philosophy of empowering the individual to have ideas, make decisions and be entrepreneurial in the running of the business.

65. Apply the Milton Model in Communication

While in Mecca talking to the King, Lawrence gets news by telegraph that Auda and some of his tribe have been in treasonous talks with the Turks. He immediately takes the boat to Aqaba to meet with the culprits and discover the truth.

> "After lunch, by pretence of sleep, I got rid of the visitors; and then abruptly asked Auda and Mohammed to walk with me to see the ruined fort and reservoir. When we were alone I touched on their present correspondence with the Turks. Auda began to laugh; Mohammed to look disgusted. At last they explained elaborately that Mohammed had taken Auda's seal and written to the Governor of Maan, offering to desert the Sherif's cause. The Turk had replied gladly, promising great rewards. Mohammed asked for something on account. Auda then heard of it, waited till the messenger with presents was on his way, caught him, robbed him to the skin: and was denying Mohammed a share of the spoils. A farcical story, and we laughed richly over it: but there was more behind.
>
> They were angry that no guns or troops had yet come to their support; and that no rewards had been given them for taking Akaba. They were anxious to know how I had learnt of their secret dealings, and how much more I knew. We were on a slippery ledge. I played on their fear by my unnecessary amusement, quoting in careless laughter, as if they were my own words, actual phrases of the letters they had exchanged. This created the impression desired."

By repeating the men's own words Lawrence is using the effective psychological techniques of anchoring and ambiguity. These relate to a set of grammatical devices called the Milton Model named after Milton Erickson, the father of modern hypnotherapy. The Milton Model is a way to make people derive meaning for themselves by hedging your language with subtle suggestive prompts and artfully vague or ambiguous phrases.

Sometimes it is useful to motivate people or unnerve opponents with embedded commands and hints like this. It's a calculated way to throw people off guard and see what their reaction is. This makes the model a very useful tool in negotiations and salesmanship.

66. Engineer Win-Wins to Secure Relationships

Lawrence subtly exposes Auda's double dealing and then works to reconcile his fears and insecurities regarding the British promises of assistance.

> "Parenthetically I told them Feisal's entire army was coming up; and how Allenby was sending rifles, guns, high explosive, food and money to Akaba. Finally I suggested that Auda's present expenses in hospitality must be great; would it help if I advanced something of the great gift Feisal would make him, personally, when he arrived? Auda saw that the immediate moment would not be unprofitable: that Feisal would be highly profitable: and that the Turks would be always with him if other resources failed. So he agreed, in a very good temper, to accept my advance: and with it to keep the Howeitat well-fed and cheerful."

Again, this is a clever use of the Milton Model by Lawrence. Non-emphasis or parenthesis is often a better vehicle for communicating an idea. An example is using negative commands such as the famous phrase, 'Don't think of an elephant.' or suggesting to someone 'You can forget that, it's not too important.' These prohibitions tend to have the opposite effect on the listener.

By knowing which buttons to press, Lawrence brings the men seamlessly back on board with casual authority. He knew the guns were the issue and he knew how to use them as a bargaining chip to get a win-win outcome. Win-wins are always necessary in negotiations where relationships, not economic costs, are the priority.

67. The Use of Spies

After patching up the cracks in the relationship and regaining the trust and commitment of Auda and Mohammed to the Arab cause, Lawrence prepares to leave for Faisal's camp, but not without some surreptitious doubling dealing of his own.

> "It was near sunset. Zaal had killed a sheep and we ate again in real amity. Afterwards I remounted, with Mufaddih (to draw Auda's allowance), and Abd el Rahman, a servant of Mohammed's who, so he whispered me, would receive any little thing I wished to send him separately. We rode all night towards Akaba, where I roused Nasir from sleep, to run over our last business."

It seems from this that Lawrence may have been playing Auda at his own game by using the servant boy as a spy to read his correspondences. I cannot advocate the use of espionage in these pages even if the end does justify the means, but it is intriguing how adept Lawrence is at using shrewdness, charm and interpersonal skills to ingratiate and manipulate people to avoid conflict and keep the organisation on track.

> 'Foreknowledge cannot be gotten from ghosts and spirits, cannot be had by analogy, cannot be found out by calculation. It must be obtained from people, people who know the conditions of the enemy.' ~ Sun-zi

Hacking is a danger that plagues businesses. Computers, phones, websites and accounts all need complex and original passwords and measures to prevent wholesale lifting of intellectual property and strategies. If you are good at what you do, it is inevitable that people will copy you and hijack your ideas. This is not necessarily a bad thing but you do need to limit the extent to which lifting takes place. Large companies have a lot of holes and places where information can be leaked even by entry level workers. Security can be overdone but lax habits and a careless attitude to the distribution of your intellectual property, systems and ideas undermines your brand and weakens your differentiation in the market.

Smart operators like Lawrence do their research and they do it by building relationships with knowledgeable people. Truth seekers are investigative by nature. They ask questions, gather data and they get in the know on a particular subject or situation by quickly acquiring a rounded understanding of it. Good entrepreneurs and executives know their market better than anyone because they speak to enough people in the industry and they speak to them regularly to swap opinions, share information and elicit facts.

68. Tradition and Continuity Mean Integrity

Lawrence describes in fine detail the social map constituting the disjointed construct of Syria. He explains that the biggest factor in bonding the people was firstly their common language and secondly a shared classical heritage.

> "A second buttress of a polity of Arab motive was the dim glory of the early Khalifate, whose memory endured among the people through centuries of Turkish misgovernment. The accident that these traditions savoured rather of the Arabian Nights than of sheer history maintained the Arab rank and file in their conviction that their past was more splendid than the present of the Ottoman Turk.
>
> Yet we knew that these were dreams. Arab Government in Syria, though buttressed on Arabic prejudices, would be as much 'imposed' as the Turkish Government, or a foreign protectorate, or the historic Caliphate. Syria remained a vividly coloured racial and religious mosaic. Any wide attempt after unity would make a patched and parcelled thing, ungrateful to a people whose instincts ever returned towards parochial home rule.
>
> Our excuse for over-running expediency was War. Syria, ripe for spasmodic local revolt, might be seethed up into insurrection, if a new factor, offering to realize that centripetal nationalism of the Beyrout Cyclopaedists, arose to restrain the jarring sects and classes. Novel the factor must be, to avoid raising a jealousy of itself: not foreign, since the conceit of Syria forbade.
>
> Within our sight the only independent factor with acceptable groundwork and fighting adherents was a Sunni prince, like Feisal, pretending to revive the glories of Ommayad or Ayubid. He might momentarily combine the inland men until success came with its need to transfer their debauched enthusiasm to the service of ordered government. Then would come reaction; but only after victory; and for victory everything material and moral might be pawned."

In order to win the hearts and minds of the Arab world, the campaign has to market itself by playing on popular nostalgia and hark back to a better time — which also happens to be the basis for modern-day jihadism. The past implies quality within the perceptions of people and products, even if it is not necessarily true. People inherently like tradition and continuity and entrepreneurs can tap into the emotions of consumers by reigniting their collective memories. The beauty of this approach is that not only does nostalgia sell, but it engenders a loyalty in customers that is hard to replicate with new concepts and brands.

> 'Borrow a corpse to resurrect the soul' ~ Chinese Proverb, *The Thirty-Six Stratagems*

69. Find Strong Metaphors

Lawrence moves from culture to geography in illustrating the mode and application of the struggle in Syria.

> "In character our operations of development for the final stroke should be like naval war, in mobility, ubiquity, independence of bases and communications, ignoring of ground features, of strategic areas, of fixed directions, of fixed points. 'He who commands the sea is at great liberty, and may take as much or as little of the war as he will.' And we commanded the desert. Camel raiding parties, self-contained like ships, might cruise confidently along the enemy's cultivation-frontier, sure of an unhindered retreat into their desert-element which the Turks could not explore."

Camels have always been known as the ships of the desert and this is one of the most enduring metaphors of Arabia. This framing of their logistical predicament was the foundation upon which Lawrence planned the campaign.

What is so interesting about Lawrence's comparison of camels and ships is that ships are a marvellous example of man's conquest over nature. Ships are relatively small, yet powerful, self-contained mobile units. They can access any part of the ocean at will, have the endurance to sail for months on end, and can weather countless storms and extreme conditions. Ships contain all the resources they need until they arrive at port, and most importantly, they are well armed so that they can travel to escape from almost any place with impunity. They can survive against all expectations. And so it is for the same reason that sailing and naval metaphors are also frequently used in business contexts.

This whole book is also based on a metaphor where I have looked at the world of business and marketing through the lens of warfare, in particular guerrilla warfare. I have used this device because metaphors allow us to see so much deeper into the matter at hand. They allow us to view problems from a different perspective and find solutions we wouldn't usually see.

Metaphors are extremely expedient heuristic devices for business people and communicators to employ. In just the same way, analogies, parables and stories also demonstrate situations in a simple way without the need for technical explanations. They resonate with the listener's inner feelings and paint a picture people can immediately identify with.

70. Pick Your Fights

The method of revolt was now clear cut in Lawrence's mind and it is one which has formed the basis of every guerrilla campaign in history.

> "Discrimination of what point of the enemy organism to disarrange would come to us with war practice. Our tactics should be tip and run: not pushes, but strokes. We should never try to improve an advantage. We should use the smallest force in the quickest time at the farthest place."

The guerrillas' tactic was to strike out of nowhere, attacking the weakest point and then disappear before the enemy had a chance to retaliate. In this way the Arabs were constantly one step ahead, always holding the initiative and almost guaranteed to come out winning every time, with minimal loss.

The asymmetric entrepreneur's metaphorical weapon of choice is the sniper rifle not the Gatling gun. Small businesses have to fight on the fronts they know they can win and avoid all else. In product development they need to fill niches. In marketing they need to eliminate wasted spending and engender maximum word of mouth reverberations. In finding and servicing clients they need to go the extra distance that other firms wouldn't even contemplate. And generally they need to be always gathering information and be on the look out for opportunities as they present themselves in real time, rather than deploying an overarching suite of permanent resources.

71. Maximise Incendiary Strikes

Lawrence describes the ability of the Bedouin to travel long distances, the limited capacity of the land for supporting men and the amount and type of weapons the Arab irregulars should possess.

> "Another distinguishing feature might be high explosives. We evolved special dynamite methods, and by the end of the war could demolish any quantity of track and bridges with economy and safety. Allenby was generous with explosive. It was only guns we never got until the last month--and the pity of it! In manoeuvre war one long-range gun outweighed ninety-nine short."

Long range guns and explosives cause maximum damage to the enemy for the least risk and effort for the raiding party. There is very little that the enemy can do to prevent them or deal with their aftermath. While the audacious train wreckings created huge publicity throughout the Middle East for Faisal's cause and for Lawrence himself, it is via this dramatic use of explosives that Lawrence starts gaining a widespread reputation as dashing and dangerous individual.

The internet is an equivalent of a long range gun in this context. This is because with the internet any individual can sell to the whole globe with minimal fuss and logistical barriers. The internet is the biggest free resource in existence. Every day opportunities crop up which allow marketers to participate in communities and provide knowledge on relevant subjects. This allows them to publicise their business either directly or indirectly. The insurgent entrepreneur, therefore, uses the internet to the maximum, aiming to dominate their industry through it.

As we saw in Lesson 63, a great way to gain attention in internet marketing is by being controversial. If you have strong opinions you are more likely to get a strong following than if you blithely sit on the fence all the time. Interesting people have solid convictions and they back them up and argue them well without getting personal, underhand or intellectually dishonest. Even if people don't agree with you, a strong opinion makes everyone sit up and take notice. Lawrence is an incendiary character. He always goes for the jugular. He doesn't hold back. He doesn't shy away from attacking the enemy and because of this people hold him in awe and his name spreads throughout the kingdom. Marketers likewise must harness a reputation that precedes them and they do it by putting their neck on the line.

72. Give People the Freedom to Do What They Are Good At

In this guerrilla war, how were the various Arab parties to form a coherent force? How were they to organise themselves and attack? Lawrence hits on a system of extreme divergence to accommodate the multitude of clans involved.

> "The distribution of the raiding parties was unorthodox. We could not mix or combine tribes, because of their distrusts: nor could we use one in the territory of another. In compensation we aimed at the widest dissipation of force; and we added fluidity to speed by using one district on Monday, another on Tuesday, a third on Wednesday. Thus natural mobility was reinforced. In pursuit, our ranks refilled with fresh men at each new tribe, and maintained the pristine energy. In a real sense maximum disorder was our equilibrium."

According to the writer and motivational speaker Dan Pink, as long as money is not a big issue among workers, people are motivated by autonomy, mastery and purpose much more than receiving more money. Autonomy means that giving people the space to do what they want, actually has unexpectedly positive consequences for a company. Likewise, allowing people the challenge to master a field of endeavour for their own satisfaction can produce amazing levels of productivity and creativity. The sense of purpose that Pink refers to means not being obsessed with profits, but pursuing a higher objective. The Arab revolt certainly had purpose. They had an over-riding philosophy of liberation in which every soldier was aware and had volunteered to fight for.

The textile manufacturer Gore-Tex is a good example. For decades they have operated as an "open allocation" organisation without managers or job titles. The employees own the company and every decision is completely democratic, organic and free from rules. As a result the company performs brilliantly, both in terms of creativity and profits. Google similarly pride themselves on constantly coming out with world-beating ideas. They employ a system where they allow staff to spend 20 per cent of the time working on their own ideas. Google let people choose want they want to do and they allow people to share equitably in its success.

All of these things are messier than the traditional uninspiring organisation with strict guidelines for individual duties and rewards, and managers who covet power. Clearly the benefits of employing a more informal and humanistic approach are worth relinquishing control for.

73. Value the Unique Individual, Not the Homogeneous Group

Furthermore, the Arabs' variety in organisation was in stark asymmetric contrast to the enemy's predictable formations.

> "The internal economy of our raiding parties achieved irregularity and extreme articulation. Our circumstances were not twice similar, so no system could fit them twice: and our diversity threw the enemy intelligence off the track. By identical battalions and divisions information built itself up, until a corps could be inferred on corpses from three companies. Our strengths depended upon whim."

Lawrence's system of accepting diversity among the Arab ranks means they were unwittingly exploiting the Law of Requisite Variety which we will come across in Chapter 11. The law states that in any system, the party which is most able to vary its behaviour to meet the circumstances that are thrown its way, is the party which is most likely to control that system. Lawrence's non-linear approach to tactics is human, personal, unfabricated, unpredictable and difficult to defeat.

Because of the Arabs' advantage in formation and deployment, they knew the Turks perfectly yet the Turks knew nothing about them. In fact, the Arabs didn't even know that much about their own strength.

The main lesson we can learn is that putting faith in the individual is a key to success. In the developed world, mechanical jobs in factories are disappearing in place of knowledge-worker office-based jobs which require thought, intelligence, creativity and interpersonal skills. Therefore a modern company ought to value individual capabilities above the raw mechanical output of faceless staff.

> 'In individuals, insanity is rare; but in groups, parties, nations and epochs, it is the rule.' ~ Nietzsche

> 'In a guerrilla war, every man is an executive.' ~ Peter Drucker

74. Let People Fight for Personal Honour and Gain

It is clear that Lawrence understands Bedouin culture. He could see the strengths and weaknesses and he could see that the nature of the Arab fighting force demanded new, more liberal, rules of engagement.

> "We were serving a common ideal, without tribal emulation, and so could not hope for Esprit de Corps. Ordinary soldiers were made a caste either by great rewards in pay, dress and privilege: or by being cut off from life by contempt. We could not so knit man to man, for our tribesmen were in arms willingly. Many armies had been voluntarily enlisted: few served voluntarily. Any of our Arabs could go home without penalty whenever the conviction failed him: the only contract was honour."

This is very much also in the spirit of history's greatest generals, summed up with typical eloquence by Machiavelli.

> 'And to the prince who goes forth with his army, supporting it by pillage, sack, and extortion, handling that which belongs to others, this liberality is necessary, otherwise he would not be followed by soldiers. And of that which is neither yours nor your subjects' you can be a ready giver, as were Cyrus, Caesar, and Alexander; because it does not take away your reputation if you squander that of others, but adds to it; it is only squandering your own that injures you.'

Lawrence's men were antagonists and pirates, willing to fight a cause that bettered their individual situations, not just in pride but in concrete monetary terms. Equally, the plunder and rewards available to sales people is a serious motivator to be used by a cash-strapped firm. When victories occur, a leader should share out the spoils so that people can see it is a democratic team which values its staff. This is in contrast to many established firms who look for every opportunity to be as stingy as possible in order to feather their own nests.

In the 'Dirty Tricks' court case between British Airways and Richard Branson, the Virgin boss won half a million pounds in compensation from BA on the grounds that they made a concerted campaign to destroy his reputation. Branson immediately distributed the winnings to his staff at HQ and organised a party. This kind of behaviour from a leader gains the greatest respect from his/her people.

75. Create a Guerrilla Army

Lawrence goes even further in turning military orthodoxy on its head to suit the insurgents' circumstances.

> "Consequently we had no discipline in the sense in which it was restrictive, submergent of individuality, the Lowest Common Denominator of men. In peace-armies discipline meant the hunt, not of an average but of an absolute; the hundred per cent standard in which the ninety-nine were played down to the level of the weakest man on parade. The aim was to render the unit a unit, the man a type; in order that their effort might be calculable, and the collective output even in grain and bulk. The deeper the discipline, the lower was the individual excellence; also the more sure the performance.
>
> By this substitution of a sure job for a possible masterpiece, military science made a deliberate sacrifice of capacity in order to reduce the uncertain element, the bionomic factor, in enlisted humanity. Discipline's necessary accompaniment was compound or social war—that form in which the fighting man was the product of the multiplied exertions of a long hierarchy, from workshop to supply unit, which kept him active in the field.
>
> The Arab war should react against this, and be simple and individual. Every enrolled man should serve in the line of battle and be self-contained there. The efficiency of our forces was the personal efficiency of the single man. It seemed to me that, in our articulated war, the sum yielded by single men would at least equal the product of a compound system of the same strength.
>
> In practice we should not employ in the firing line the great numbers which a simple system put theoretically at our disposal, lest our attack (as contrasted with our threat) become too extended. The moral strain of isolated fighting made 'simple' war very hard upon the soldier, exacting from him special initiative, endurance, enthusiasm. Irregular war was far more intellectual than a bayonet charge, far more exhausting than service in the comfortable imitative obedience of an ordered army. Guerillas

must be allowed liberal work room: in irregular war, of two men together, one was being wasted. Our ideal should be to make our battle a series of single combats, our ranks a happy alliance of agile commanders-in-chief."

This is an elegant reaction to the Total War doctrines of Clausewitz which dominated the 19th century. Lawrence's adventures in the Arab Revolt captured the imaginations of the British people because they were in such contrast to the idiocy of the Great War in Europe where massive amounts of resources were wasted resulting in enormous casualties with little or no gain.

In many ways Lawrence was following in the footsteps of Alexander the Great, not least by using the brilliant technique of reframing problems to suit his situation; turning a disadvantage into an advantage and a weakness into a strength. His campaign harked back to an earlier time when fighting was of a more individualist, swashbuckling and glorious nature.

Lawrence was really the first person to critically define the concept of guerrilla war. The original term, guerrilla, came from the Peninsula War fought by Wellington in Portugal and Spain against the French. During this conflict the indigenous Spanish resistance was so logistically and numerically weak against Napoleon's Army that they had to employ highly secretive and heavily sabotaging tactics to maximise their effect and cripple the invaders.

Guerrilla marketers and negotiators in weak positions must use the twin elements of secrecy and surprise to fight on an even keel — putting the open resources of time and space to better use than the relatively static opposition. Advertising budgets and manpower can be decisively conquered by niche-filling innovation, relationship management, intelligence, inspiration, loyalty, good timing and future opportunities, all of which are fair game to the usurping enterprise.

But above all, the guerrilla marketer must be a populist who wants to make the market a better place for consumers whose needs have for too long been ignored by the existing power structures.

'Why does the guerrilla fighter fight? We must come to the inevitable conclusion that the guerrilla fighter is a social reformer, that he takes up arms responding to the angry protest of the people against their oppressors.' ~ Che Guevara

76. Always Think Ahead

During their time at Aqaba, the Arabs carry out incessant pin-prick raids against the Turks entrenched at Ma'an while the British deliver a devastating bombing campaign from the air. Lawrence resolves to intensify the training-wrecking enterprise.

> "Of targets, the most promising and easiest-reached seemed Mudowwara, a water station eighty miles south of Maan. A smashed train there would embarrass the enemy. For men, I would have the tried Howeitat; and, at the same time, the expedition would test the three Haurani peasants whom I had added to my personal followers. In view of the new importance of the Hauran, there was need for us to learn its dialect, the construction and jealousies of its clan-framework, and its names and roads. These three fellows, Rahail, Assaf and Hemeid would teach me their home-affairs imperceptibly, as we rode on business, chatting."

Lawrence delights in learning and gathering intelligence for the future fight. He is a first class scholar and displays the keenest intellect in cultural and political affairs. Leaders in every field need to stay one step ahead and they do this with an understanding of the fact that knowledge is power. Most people don't plan ahead and thus they fall at the first test.

To complement this didactic thirst, Lawrence is always on the lookout for opportunities — the more daring and ambitious the better. It is both audacious and sensible to attack a train rather than just destroy the track. His aim was to keep the railway functioning but only just. This created maximum disruption and irritance while stalling time — with the knowledge that there would be a point in the future when the Allies were ready enough to commandeer the line themselves.

77. Don't Take Undue Risks

After an arduous journey through the famous Rum Valley and having to smooth over mutinous factions dangerously testing their unity, they finally arrive by night at the enemy station.

> "We moved back to our hill and consulted in whispers. The station was very long, of stone buildings, so solid that they might be proof against our time-fused shell. The garrison seemed about two hundred. We were one hundred and sixteen rifles and not a happy family. Surprise was the only benefit we could be sure of.
>
> So, in the end, I voted that we leave it, unalarmed, for a future occasion, which might be soon. But, actually, one accident after another saved Mudowwara; and it was not until August, 1918, that Buxton's Camel Corps at last measured to it the fate so long overdue."

Guerrillas only fight when they can be sure of winning. They are willing to call off an attack at the slightest sign of being compromised. Taking risks is necessary and indeed a positive behaviour but taking undue risks is just plain reckless. Caution is the better part of valour and exercising your judgement needs to be done in a cold and sober light away from the intoxicating crest of emotion and creativity.

Your intuition is a valuable guide in decision making but intuition should be used as a guide rather than an absolute answer to something. Despite the desire to attack, reason came down heavier against it and Lawrence had the clarity of vision to see it.

78. Model and Repeat Successful Behaviour

At Mudawwara they blow a train to pieces and return to Aqaba gloriously laden with spoils.

> "Days passed, talking politics, organization and strategy with Feisal, while preparations for a new operation went forward. Our luck had quickened the camp; and the mining of trains promised to become popular, if we were able to train in the technique of the work enough men for several parties. Captain Pisani was first volunteer. He was the experienced commander of the French at Akaba, an active soldier who burned for distinction--and distinctions. Feisal found me three young Damascenes of family, who were ambitious to lead tribal raids. We went to Rumm and announced that this raid was specially for Gasim's clan. Such coals of fire scorched them; but greed would not let them refuse. Everyone for days around flocked to join. Most were denied: nevertheless, we started out with one hundred and fifty men and a huge train of empty pack-camels for the spoils."

Lawrence has now become the principal hero of the revolt and he is eager to take a full leadership role. He wants to spread his ideas and put his aims into action. He is demonstrating an implicit awareness of the following two central precepts in Neuro Linguistic Programming.

> 'If you keep doing what you are doing, you will keep getting what you are getting.'

> 'If one person can learn to do something, anyone can learn to do it.'

The art of train mining was systematically disseminated at Aqaba with such a zest that over the next four months seventeen locomotives were destroyed. This crippled the Turks. It wrecked their logistical and territorial control over Palestine and the Hejaz and accounted for the loss of massive amounts of property taken off as booty. The Arabs not only armed but educated their people continually so that every lowliest soldier knew the aims, the system and the methods to be employed.

Chapter VII

Lessons 79 — 86

Handling Adversity

Raid upon the Bridges — Précis

Now the strengthened British Army in Egypt are eager to hit the Turks to put them beyond the fight for good. However, Lawrence has reservations about whether this is the right time for the Arabs to go all out for victory. He plumps for the middle ground by resolving to venture deep into Syria to blow up one of the enemy's main bridges and cut off their avenue of retreat from the British. With a small band of men including two new British sappers and a group of Indian machine gunners, he sets out on another furtive foray into the beautiful and foreboding wilderness. At night to the west they can hear the British guns pounding away in Palestine. As the sojourn continues they begin to fall into an increasingly disadvantageous position not least by the fact that a foolish Algerian prince travelling with them is lost and defects to the Turks. Just as they are about to dynamite the bridge in the dead of night the party are discovered and a firefight ensues. The men beat a hasty retreat and are chased for miles.

Rather than return to camp as failures the group resolve to blow up a train. Lawrence lightens the team by sending sick and tired men home as the winter begins to draw in. With their spirits close to breaking point they prepare for one more swipe at the railway and after dangerously failing on the first attempt they succeed on the second. By sheer luck they hit the train carrying one of the Turkish leaders, Ahmed Djemal Pasha, on his way to command his army against the British.

After this Lawrence goes into winter quarters at the ancient northern fort of Azraq. As the winter begins to bite and the men are stuck in their fort, Lawrence determines to venture out with a Syrian guide intent on surveying the land in preparation for the coming rising in the spring. While scouting an enemy station at Deera he is captured and enrolled into service in the Turkish Army, whereby he is beaten and whipped to within an inch of his life. The next day Lawrence promptly escapes, all the while protecting his identity and in the end finding out the hard way everything he needed to know about the next target of the campaign.

Unsatisfied with sedentary life at camp surrounded by sycophants and with the weather taking its toll on his spirits, Lawrence heads south on a long and brutal ride to Aqaba. When he arrives at the camp he is ordered meet Allenby in Gaza and flies to Palestine to prepare for the pomp-filled British entry into Jerusalem.

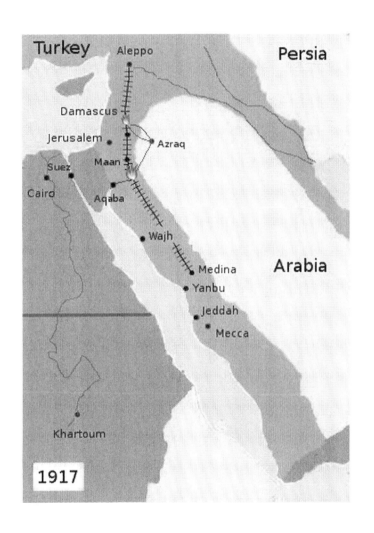

"By November, 1917, Allenby was ready to open a general attack against the Turks along his whole front. The Arabs should have done the same in their sector: but I was afraid to put everything on a throw, and designed instead the specious operation of cutting the Yarmuk valley railway, to throw into disorder the expected Turkish retreat. This half-measure met with the failure it deserved."

Lessons 79 — 86

Handling Adversity

79. Integrate into the Local Community

Lawrence describes the British change of high command in Egypt and their intricately renewed plans to defeat the Turks in Palestine. Meanwhile the Arabs had no such difficulty.

> "We on the Arab front were very intimate with the enemy. Our Arab officers had been Turkish Officers, and knew every leader on the other side personally. They had suffered the same training, thought the same, took the same point of view. By practising modes of approach upon the Arabs we could explore the Turks: understand, almost get inside, their minds. Relation between us and them was universal, for the civil population of the enemy area was wholly ours without pay or persuasion. In consequence our intelligence service was the widest, fullest and most certain imaginable."

Leaders need the help of people and communities as resources to provide knowledge of the opponents' practices, ideas, and philosophies. This especially includes former employees. Be fully tuned-in to your opponent strategically and intellectually by networking and enquiring as much as you can.

A manager can pretend that he knows his market but he never really knows it until he actually gets out of his office and goes and interacts with his actual clientele. You must do the leg work to have any hope of controlling your field. This is such a hard thing for most managers to because it is much more enticing to delegate that task and take an academic perspective of the industry.

Too many people, once they reach the echelons of management, seek to avoid the 'real' work that they were used to. This attitude springs from a lack of passion coupled with a heightened sense of self-importance. The problem is that people who fool themselves that they actually know what is going on in the market are the ones who are least likely to foresee or cope with changes when they do occur.

80. Look for Areas of Complacency in Your Opponent

Intending to assist the British, Lawrence targets two key bridges in the Yarmouk Valley in modern-day Jordan.

> "To cut either of these bridges would isolate the Turkish army in Palestine, for one fortnight, from its base in Damascus, and destroy its power of escaping from Allenby's advance. To reach the Yarmuk we should need to ride from Akaba, by way of Azrak, some four hundred and twenty miles. The Turks thought the danger from us so remote that they guarded the bridges insufficiently.
>
> Accordingly we suggested the scheme to Allenby, who asked that it be done on November the fifth, or one of the three following days. If it succeeded, and the weather held up afterwards for a fortnight, the odds were that no coherent unit of von Rress's army would survive its retreat to Damascus. The Arabs would then have their opportunity to carry their wave forward into the great capital, taking up at the half-way point from the British, whose original impulse would then be nearly exhausted, with the exhaustion of their transport."

The lesson here is to attack where people least expect it — which is where they can be least defended. Not only does this hit your enemy unexpectedly, it hits them where it really hurts. Fortune favours the brave and the rewards in such an outrageous attack usually greatly outweigh the risks.

This is exactly what Apple did with the iPhone. They saw a well-established market which producers and consumers had assumed to be ticking along just fine, where everyone had become unwittingly satisfied with what they had. Then Steve Jobs came from nowhere and gave people something so new and revolutionary that it made what had gone before look practically prehistoric. Jobs attacked the market from such a different angle that he took everyone by surprise and blew the competition out of the water. Only he had the extraordinary vision and drive to do something different and move the world forward.

Entrepreneurs have to search for products and territories where their competition has fooled themselves into believing they are dominant but in reality have been resting on their laurels for too long. The paradox we saw in Lesson 34 is that the greater your ambition, the greater your chance of success. People worry about not being able to compete in an industry dominated by big established players, but the guerrilla knows that there is always space in badly serviced markets, and there will always be enough of those, even if the whole market doesn't realise it yet...

81. People Smart is Better than Book Smart

While riding with the famous Beni Sakhr tribe, Lawrence strains to learn their dialect and keep up with the gossip and hierarchies surrounding tribal affairs.

> "In the little-peopled desert every worshipful man knew every other; and instead of books they studied their generation. To have fallen short in such knowledge would have meant being branded either as ill-bred, or as a stranger; and strangers were not admitted to familiar intercourse or councils, or confidences. There was nothing so wearing, yet nothing so important for the success of my purpose, as this constant mental gymnastic of apparent omniscience at each time of meeting a new tribe."

Business is not about balance sheets, book-knowledge, marketing, technology or organisation so much as it is about people. This is what is meant when people say that EQ is more important than IQ. Relationships are worth more than knowledge in business and that is not to say that being erudite is not helpful, but being urbane is even more so.

Many great CEOs and political leaders have got to the top not by having wonderful education credentials but by having exceptional communication and people skills. Many great writers have had little formal education and certainly not studied English at Oxford or Cambridge, but have had a wealth of life experience that allows them to form extensive opinions and thoughts on almost any matters worth talking about.

Ultimately this comes down to empathy and social skills — being able to recognise and manage not only your own emotions but the emotions of others. One of the big advantages of EQ over IQ is that a person's measured intelligence is largely a fixed matter from the moment of birth. On the other hand, a person's emotional intelligence can be developed and matured through regular training. This education in people skills and people knowledge is a course of action that Lawrence and any ambitious person is more than willing to undertake.

82. Live Each Day As If It's Your Last

On the way to Azraq they encounter a group of fighting men from the influential Serahin tribe. Consequently the party pay a visit to the tribal camp where, with some difficulty, they implore them to support the raid and the wider mission to aid Allenby.

> "We put it to them, not abstractedly, but concretely, for their case, how life in mass was sensual only, to be lived and loved in its extremity. There could be no rest-houses for revolt, no dividend of joy paid out. Its spirit was accretive, to endure as far as the senses would endure, and to use each such advance as base for further adventure, deeper privation, sharper pain. Sense could not reach back or forward. A felt emotion was a conquered emotion, an experience gone dead, which we buried by expressing it.
>
> To be of the desert was, as they knew, a doom to wage unending battle with an enemy who was not of the world, nor life, nor anything, but hope itself; and failure seemed God's freedom to mankind. We might only exercise this our freedom by not doing what it lay within our power to do, for then life would belong to us, and we should have mastered it by holding it cheap. Death would seem best of all our works, the last free loyalty within our grasp, our final leisure: and of these two poles, death and life, or, less finally, leisure and subsistence, we should shun subsistence (which was the stuff of life) in all save its faintest degree, and cling close to leisure. Thereby we would serve to promote the not-doing rather than the doing. Some men, there might be, uncreative; whose leisure was barren; but the activity of these would have been material only. To bring forth immaterial things, things creative, partaking of spirit, not of flesh, we must be jealous of spending time or trouble upon physical demands, since in most men the soul grew aged long before the body. Mankind had been no gainer by its drudges.
>
> There could be no honour in a sure success, but much might be wrested from a sure defeat. Omnipotence and the Infinite were our two worthiest foemen, indeed the only ones for a full man to meet, they being monsters of his own spirit's making; and the

stoutest enemies were always of the household. In fighting Omnipotence, honour was proudly to throw away the poor resources that we had, and dare Him empty-handed; to be beaten, not merely by more mind, but by its advantage of better tools. To the clear-sighted, failure was the only goal. We must believe, through and through, that there was no victory, except to go down into death fighting and crying for failure itself, calling in excess of despair to Omnipotence to strike harder, that by His very striking He might temper our tortured selves into the weapon of His own ruin."

To paraphrase Tennyson, it is better to have lived and died than to never have been born at all. This is a fundamental asymmetrical proposition that embodies the ideals of the campaign. With a profound speech Lawrence persuades the tribesmen not to be limited by their normal expectations of life but to strain every sinew to achieve the impossible.

We must go to extremes to win and sometimes your business must encompass the whole of your life, as mentioned in Lesson 11. Sometimes work goals must be your driving force and raison d'etre. Machiavelli discusses the quality of leaders through the remarkable example of Ferdinand of Aragon, the Spanish King famous for sponsoring Christopher Columbus. He demonstrates that success in one area should lay the foundation for further success in subsequent ventures constituting an unstoppable rise to greatness.

> 'Under this same cloak he assailed Africa, he came down on Italy, he has finally attacked France; and thus his achievements and designs have always been great, and have kept the minds of his people in suspense and admiration and occupied with the issue of them. And his actions have arisen in such a way, one out of the other, that men have never been given time to work steadily against him.'

In order to achieve such connected achievements we must live life to the full. Success may be painful but we all need to lead meaningful lives on this earth and that means going beyond what is expected of us.

83. Don't Tolerate In-fighting

After reaching the ancient and deserted fort at Azraq, they get acquainted with their surroundings, settle in and plan for the coming attack on the bridge.

> "Unhappily my rest time was spoiled by a bed of justice. The feud between Ahmed and Awad broke out during this gazelle chase into a duel. Awad shot off Ahmed's head-rope; Ahmed holed Awad's cloak. I disarmed them and gave loud order that the right thumb and forefinger of each be cut off. The terror of this drove them into an instant, violent and public kissing of peace. A little later all my men went capital bail that the trouble had ended. I referred the case to Ali ibn el Hussein, who set them at liberty on probation, after sealing their promise with the ancient and curious nomad penance of striking the head sharply with the edge of a weighty dagger again and again till the issuing blood had run down to the waist belt. It caused painful but not dangerous scalp wounds, whose ache at first and whose scars later were supposed to remind the would-be defaulter of the bond he had given."

Ill discipline and in-fighting must be dealt with remorselessly and quickly to nip it in the bud. In-fighting weakens a team's morale and purpose — it is a cancer that cannot be allowed to fester. Often the shock of such a severe punishment can be enough to bring both parties back to normal so that the actual retribution does not have to be so harsh in the end.

Organisations can never really avoid political splits, disputes and allegiances but they can certainly be minimised and neutralised by senior managers keeping an unbiased eye on the dynamics and emergent power structures within the group. Not being aloof or distant, but a leader who speaks to people at all levels and unifies them, goes a long way to stamping out disharmony.

84. Put Your House in Good Order

Despite the failure of the attack on the bridge, they eventually manage to mine a train. After this they retire to Azraq Castle, hunker down in winter quarters and fortify their position.

> "So I established myself in its southern gate-tower, and set my six Haurani boys (for whom manual labour was not disgraceful) to cover with brushwood, palm-branches, and clay the ancient split stone rafters, which stood open to the sky. Ali took up his quarters in the south-east corner tower, and made that roof tight. The Indians weather-proofed their own north-west rooms. We arranged the stores on the ground floor of the western tower, by the little gate, for it was the soundest, driest place. The Biasha chose to live under me in the south gate. So we blocked that entry and made a hall of it. Then we opened a great arch from the court to the palm-garden, and made a ramp, that our camels might come inside each evening.
>
> Hassan Shah we appointed Seneschal. As a good Moslem his first care was for the little mosque in the square. It had been half unroofed and the Arabs had penned sheep within the walls. He set his twenty men to dig out the filth, and wash the pavement clean. The mosque then became a most attractive house of prayer. What had been a place shut off, dedicated to God alone, Time had broken open to the Evanescent with its ministering winds and rain and sunlight; these entering into the worship taught worshippers how the two were one.
>
> Our prudent Jemadar's next labour was to make positions for machine-guns in the upper towers, from whose tops the approaches lay at mercy. Then he placed a formal sentry (a portent and cause of wonder in Arabia) whose main duty was the shutting of the postern gate at sundown. The door was a poised slab of dressed basalt, a foot thick, turning on pivots of itself, socketed into threshold and lintel. It took a great effort to start swinging, and at the end went shut with a clang and crash which made tremble the west wall of the old castle."

Lawrence fixed up Azraq, a ramshackle ruined dwelling, but boasting an ancient and famous spiritual heritage, into a functioning base from which to preach the revolution, stabilise the movement and plan for victory.

In business it's important to look at old resources and use them as vehicles and inspiration for future growth. This might include taking old projects and ideas out of mothballs, re-establishing old contacts, reinventing old products and reviving forgotten marketing practices. When things go out of fashion or become defunct, it is often an indication they will become useful again at some time in the future. As mentioned in Lesson 68, there is a Chinese idiom from the classic military text *The Thirty-Six Strategies*, which states that in a time of war a general should 'find a dead body to resurrect its soul.' The protagonist must look to the past to find an ideological shelter for his cause, returning buildings, institutions, products or practices to their former glory, breathing life into them for his own purposes.

Later on in the campaign, Azraq Castle swelled to become the crucial launching place for the push into Damascus. An entrepreneur and innovator must be shrewd enough to find space with potential and make it a base. Often the best method of doing this is to rent an office in a slightly run-down but sufficiently central part of town which will rise in the future as the surrounding areas develop. By doing this you don't pay a premium but you do profit in future years.

85. Build It, and They Will Come

As news of the victors' new camp spreads, the fort turns into a regional headquarters.

> "Then began our flood of visitors. All day and every day they came, now in the running column of shots, raucous shouting and rush of camel-feet which meant a Bedouin parade, it might be of Rualla, or Sherarat, or Serahin, Serdiyeh, or Beni Sakhr, chiefs of great name like ibn Zuhair, ibn Kaebir, Rafa el Khoreisha, or some little father of a family demonstrating his greedy goodwill before the fair eyes of Ali ibn el Hussein. Then it would be a wild gallop of horse: Druses, or the ruffling warlike peasants of the Arab plain. Sometimes it was a cautious, slow-led caravan of ridden camels, from which stiffly dismounted Syrian politicians or traders not accustomed to the road. One day arrived a hundred miserable Armenians, fleeing starvation and the suspended terror of the Turks. Again would come a spick and span group of mounted officers, Arab deserters from the Turkish armies, followed, often as not, by a compact company of Arab rank and file. Always they came, day after day, till the desert, which had been trackless when we came, was starred out with grey roads."

As a new business owner, if your product is a genuinely good one, and you have done enough promotion, and everything in your power to prepare, then you don't have to worry about getting a following.

Lawrence benefits from a great deal of word-of-mouth advertising — which is a much sought after phenomenon for businesses because it constitutes the most effective form of marketing. If you can get people to speak positively about your service in a social context then not only do you pay nothing for the privilege but you get the biggest impact possible. We trust the word of our peers — whom we believe are speaking from honest opinion and not being incentivised by the firm itself.

A 'tipping point' is a consequent social phenomenon with big ramifications in marketing. It occurs when a new product or idea has a slow initial take up; like a new fashion that makes the few people who wear it stand out as quirky and odd, yet after a time the fashion catches on and take-up accelerates until it becomes the norm.

If your product is genuinely good but new, then it may take a lot of protracted effort and promotion to get it adopted to this point of critical mass, where momentum allows it to market itself. It is natural for people to be behind the bell curve; to ignore, criticise and fear positive change, but the insurgent entrepreneur can have faith that after hardship comes the reward.

> 'I have found out one thing and that is, if you have an idea, and it is a good idea, if you only stick to it you will come out all right.' ~ Cecil Rhodes

86. If in Doubt, Bluff Your Way Out

Frustrated by the clamour and attention at Azraq, Lawrence strikes out to the south on a scouting mission to the Dead Sea area. On the first night, they halt in terrible conditions and come under attack from a raiding party.

> "Suddenly shots rang out at close range, and four mouthing men dashed down the slope towards us. I stopped my camel peaceably. Seeing this they jumped off, and ran to us brandishing their arms. They asked who I was: volunteering that they were Jazi Howietat.
>
> This was an open lie, because their camel-brands were Faiz. They covered us with rifles at four yards, and told us to dismount. I laughed at them, which was good tactics with Beduin at a crisis. They were puzzled. I asked the loudest if he knew his name. He stared at me, thinking I was mad. He came nearer, with his finger on the trigger, and I bent down to him and whispered that it must be 'Teras' since no other tradesman could be so rude. As I spoke, I covered him with a pistol hidden under my cloak.
>
> It was a shooting insult, but he was so astonished that anyone should provoke an armed man, as to give up for the moment his thought of murdering us. He took a step back, and looked around, fearful that there was a reserve somewhere, to give us confidence. At once I rode off slowly, with a creepy feeling in my back, calling Rahail to follow. They let him go too, unhurt. When we were a hundred yards away, they repented themselves, and began to shoot, but we dashed over the watershed into the next depression, and across it cantered more confidently into safe ground."

When negotiating with a client, especially an unknown or potential client who you feel is challenging you, never show the slightest weakness, but always be thinking quickly. Like a swan, Lawrence is graceful on the surface but paddling furiously below. If you behave with absolute surety, it wrong-foots and unnerves potential aggressors because they expect a reaction.

Not giving people the satisfaction of seeing a negative reaction in you is the key to dealing with all conflict. If people are rude, aggressive or downright mean you have to avoid negative reciprocation, no matter how difficult and unnerving it may be for you at the time. The more negative your opposite numbers become, the more polite and positive you have to become; always remembering Einstein's dictum that a problem cannot be solved at the same level of thinking that created it. This means that the solution to dealing with difficult people is to show more empathy than they do while acting in a more professional way they do. In this way you shame them into submission on two fronts.

In non-combative interactions the reverse of this practice can be adopted by surprising people with self-deprecation to break the ice, create humour, friendliness and trust. Many people go into any sort of formal interactions with a degree of nerves and apprehension. The good communicator is aware of this and is able to effortlessly dispel awkwardness, mistrust and negative energy before it has a chance to rear its head and cause problems. You can't always prevent problems from happening, but you can always control your reactions and to an extent, other people's reactions, to those problems.

Chapter VIII

Lessons 87 — 97

Changing the Status Quo

The Dead Sea Campaign — Précis

The Arabs' new goal in the spring of 1918 was to move north into Palestine and stop the flow of Turkish supplies along the Dead Sea. During the winter the Turks had been crippled by Arab incursions and Lawrence and a team of British soldiers had driven their Roll Royce armoured cars up to Mudawwara and destroyed the Turkish post there. Lawrence now has a price of twenty-thousand pounds on his head and so he enlists an elite bodyguard of ninety ruthless men, who ride everywhere with him.

The new campaign begins well with a successful attack against Jurf, in which a great amount of booty is captured. Next Shobak falls as the Turks flee panic-stricken straight into Arab gunfire. After that the village of Tafilah surrenders and the Arabs prepare their next targets. But then suddenly without warning, the Turks counterattack and to try and recapture the insignificant village. They fail miserably as the Arabs stand their ground and slaughter the Turks at the end of a day of hard fighting. Three days later, this is followed by the swift sinking of the Turkish Navy by an Arab cavalry charge on the Dead Sea's northern harbour. Thus comes the surprise early-completion of the Dead Sea mission by the end of January 1918. Lawrence then breaks up the miserable winter camp at Tafilah and goes in search of more money and men for the coming campaign in the north of Jordan. The short but gruelling march to Quweira through the hills in the cold, wind and rain, killed all except one of the camels and nearly killed the men themselves.

After a few days rest in the comfort of the camp, Lawrence begins the equally arduous return journey. By this time the British were already in the Jordan Valley heading for the Turkish-controlled town of Jericho. At Tafilah Lawrence finds that Faisal's brother, Zeid, has foolishly spent his share of the war gold in paying off various contingents. This means that further incursions are impossible and Lawrence has no option but to quit the revolt with haste and rejoin Allenby.

Back in Palestine, a conference among the western Allies was convening to which Lawrence was asked to share his views on future strategy. It is agreed that the Arabs will continue the fight up into Jordan so that the Allies may rapidly take Damascus and Allenby can then return to the

European theatre where he was needed in the stalemate that was being played out. In the first phase of the operation the Arabs would attack the Turkish stronghold at Ma'an, where the railway ended. The British would then drive through the Jordan Valley and cut the railway for good.

As usual after much soul searching, Lawrence ends the chapter in an optimistic flurry as he returns to a despairing Faisal in Aqaba with the news that Allenby has credited him with three hundred thousand pounds and a large supply of camels, men and equipment. Tafilah was retaken a week later by the Turks but this insignificant if embarrassing loss meant that the enemy forces around Ma'an and Amman would now be somewhat weaker.

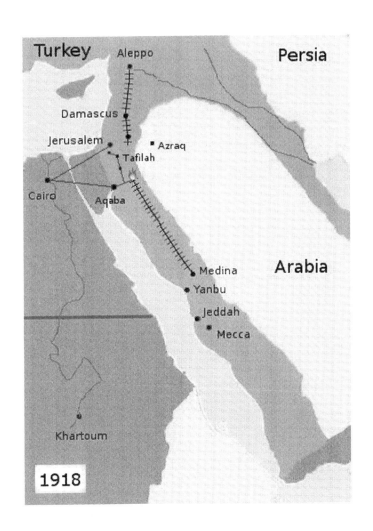

"After the capture of Jerusalem, Allenby, to relieve his right, assigned us a limited objective. We began well; but when we reached the Dead Sea, bad weather, bad temper and division of purpose blunted our offensive spirit and broke up our force.

I had a misunderstanding with Zeid, threw in my hand, and returned to Palestine reporting that we had failed, and asking the favour of other employment. Allenby was in the hopeful midst of a great scheme for the coming spring. He sent me back at once to Feisal with new powers and duties."

Lessons 87 — 97

Changing the Status Quo

87. Never Complain and Never Explain

Back at Aqaba, Lawrence and a small group of British soldiers race their eight armoured cars into the desert on a mission to pound the enemy positions.

> "This section was an oddment, which General Clayton had seen in Egypt, and had sent down to us in an inspired moment. Its Talbots, specially geared for heavy work, carried two ten-pounders with British gunners. It was wicked to give good men such rotten tools; yet their spirit seemed hardly affected by the inferior weapons. Their commander, Brodie, was a silent Scotsman, never very buoyant and never too anxious; a man who found difficulties shameful to notice, and who stamped himself on his fellows. However hard the duty given them, they always attacked it with such untroubled determination that their will prevailed. On every occasion and in every crisis they would be surely in place at their moment, perspiring but imperturbable, with never a word in explanation or complaint."

'Never complain, never explain' is a famous quote by British Prime Minister, Benjamin Disraeli. It highlights the need for leaders to be steadfast at all times and not be swayed by the opinions of others, or habitually make excuses and harbour subjective and futile reactions to challenging situations.

Wise leaders are stoic in nature. They do not get overjoyed too easily and they do not become dismayed in the face of difficulty or get frustrated with things which lie outside their control. Instead, good leaders are resolute in their course of action even if in hindsight that decision turns out to be a mistaken one. Successful people are equally resolute in their determination to make the best of bad situations. Like the British troops, they are confidently reliant in the knowledge that their own experience and expertise will see them through.

88. Don't Let Sentimentality Cloud Your Judgment

The armoured vehicles with their impervious strength in attack proved to be a game-changing addition which served not only to beat, but humiliate the Turks.

> "The certainty that in a day from Guweira we could be operating along the railway, meant that traffic lay at our mercy. All the Turks in Arabia could not fight a single armoured car in open country. Thereby the situation of Medina, already bad, became hopeless. The German Staff saw it, and after Falkenhayn's visit to Maan, they repeatedly urged abandonment of everything south of that point; but the old Turk party valued Medina as the last remnant of their sovereignty in the Holy Places, their surviving claim upon the Caliphate. Sentiment swung them to the decision, against military expediency."

Medina is the spiritual capital of Arabia, enshrined with history and significance. The Turks were desperate to hold on to the city because of its symbolic value. Lesson 68 dealt with the positive side of nostalgia and continuity in marketing. However, using an outdated schema for management and an over-belief in the importance of history can turn your cause into an unrealistic and even fanciful ideal.

The Turks' desperate clutching to the past was an intellectually dishonest strategy which did not help their overall cause and greatly weakened their position. They were still envisioning the glory of their empire and failing to adapt to the present times. They refused to view the war in the cold light of reality. Their commanders wanted to fight in an orthodox way which resonated with their contrived ideal while they ignored the nature of the actual conflict on the ground. It is for this reason they were widely beaten.

89. Make a Name for Yourself

The Turkish command, infuriated with British influence in the Arab Revolt, put a bounty on Lawrence's head.

> "However, the Turks said it often enough to make it an article of faith, and began to offer a reward of one hundred pounds for a British officer alive or dead. As time went on they not only increased the general figure, but made a special bid for me. After the capture of Akaba the price became respectable; while after we blew up Jemal Pasha they put Ali and me at the head of their list; worth twenty thousand pounds alive or ten thousand dead."

This lesson shows that to win, you can't hide your light under a bushel. Lawrence keeps a high profile and becomes such a nuisance to the opposition that they all know of him.

Entrepreneurs must seek to create an enigma and build a reputation. Sometimes you have to antagonise the big players a bit so that you get noticed. With the internet it is easy to fight a corner like this. All you need to create your own online PR department is a blog and other social platforms to interact with your community. The trick, when communicating with fellow professionals, competitors and customers, is to always be civilised and only cause a storm when you need to make a point. As long as you keep doing what you do best and talking about it as a true expert, you'll get the publicity you need.

90. Build a Team of Desperadoes

For his own safety, Lawrence forms a personal bodyguard.

> "Of course, the offer was rhetorical; with no certainty whether in gold or paper, or that the money would be paid at all. Still, perhaps, it might justify some care. I began to increase my people to a troop, adding such lawless men as I found, fellows whose dash had got them into trouble elsewhere. I needed hard riders and hard livers; men proud of themselves, and without family. By good fortune three or four of this sort joined me at the first, setting a tone and standard."

The first recruits are all important. They create a model for future staff members and they say a lot about your business. Ideally you want a team full of characters who are 'seize the day' types. Even if some of your salespeople and creatives are slightly wild, that is preferable to having boring people working for you. Wild people are original and have a lot of life experience. A good manager should take pride in harnessing their energies through good man-management.

In *Henry V*, Shakespeare describes the transformation of Prince Hal from a roguish drunkard into a brilliant and respected leader with the following analogy.

> 'The strawberry grows underneath the nettle,
> And wholesome berries thrive and ripen best
> Neighbour'd by fruit of baser quality;
> And so the Prince obscured his contemplation
> Under the veil of wildness, which, no doubt,
> Grew like the summer grass, fastest by night,
> Unseen yet crescive in his faculty.'
> This describes perfectly the path of many great men.'

Lawrence understood that people can mature by putting aside their foolish former ways and actually be all the stronger by coming from the wrong side of the tracks.

91. Turn Your Team into an Elite Force

The bodyguard developed a unique culture and a tight esprit de corps within their unit.

> "I paid my men six pounds a month, the standard army wage for a man and camel, but mounted them on my own animals, so that the money was clear income: this made the service enviable, and put the eager spirits of the camp at my disposal. For my timetable's sake, since I was more busy than most, my rides were long, hard and sudden. The ordinary Arab, whose camel represented half his wealth, could not afford to founder it by travelling my speed: also such riding was painful for the man.
>
> [...]
>
> Fellows were very proud of being in my bodyguard, which developed a professionalism almost flamboyant. They dressed like a bed of tulips, in every colour but white; for that was my constant wear, and they did not wish to seem to presume. In half an hour they would make ready for a ride of six weeks, that being the limit for which food could be carried at the saddle-bow. Baggage camels they shrank from as a disgrace. They would travel day and night at my whim, and made it a point of honour never to mention fatigue. If a new man grumbled, the others would silence him, or change the current of his complaint, brutally. They fought like devils, when I wanted, and sometimes when I did not, especially with Turks or with outsiders. For one guardsman to strike another was the last offence. They expected extravagant reward and extravagant punishment. They made boast throughout the army of their pains and gains. By this unreason in each degree they were kept apt for any effort, any risk."

Lawrence followed Napoleon and Caesar's example by creating a special unit of extraordinary individuals who set themselves apart from the rank and file. The bodyguard prided themselves on being the most well-trained and toughest men. Lawrence paid them well and received their devoted loyalty. At the same time, he fostered an unbeatable spirit of camaraderie so that his men were genuinely proud to be part of his team and go the extra mile.

92. Foster Internal Competition

The Arab spirit made the men difficult to command but their tribal feuds kept them naturally divided and this enabled Lawrence to lead them more effectively.

> "However, for the time the Arabs were possessed, and cruelty of governance answered their need. Besides, they were blood enemies of thirty tribes, and only for my hand over them would have murdered in the ranks each day. Their feuds prevented them combining against me; while their unlikeness gave me sponsors and spies wherever I went or sent, between Akaba and Damascus, between Beersheba and Bagdad. In my service nearly sixty of them died."

Lesson 83 discussed the dangers of in-fighting but at the same time, there is value in keeping your team ever so slightly divided to encourage healthy competition and in the process encourage staff to rally to you as a leader.

Abraham Lincoln inducted his political enemies into his cabinet after he was elected. He did this because he knew they would be safer inside than out. They would focus their energies on surpassing each other for his favour rather than going against him directly. Unlike some managers, he wasn't afraid of strong and competent people below him. If you enfranchise your enemies or potential enemies they cease to become enemies and then you can really benefit from their abilities.

93. Turn Enemies into Friends

The New Year brought a flurry of Arab victories in battles along the line to the south of the Dead Sea. At the key town of Tafilah, Faisal's brother Zeid, has to conciliate between two bitterly rival factions and bring the hostile party on board the Arab Revolt.

> "Zeid thanked and paid Auda and sent him back to his desert. The enlightened heads of the Muhaisin had to go as forced guests to Feisal's tent. Dhiab, their enemy, was our friend: we remembered regretfully the adage that the best allies of a violently-successful new regime were not its partisans, but its opponents. By Zeid's plenty of gold the economic situation improved. We appointed an officer-governor and organized our five villages for further attack."

The magnanimous Arabs were more than willing to allow former Turkish adherents into their fold. This is one of the oldest rules of statesmanship, elucidated by Machiavelli and exemplified by Lincoln.

In the state of flux which defines interpersonal affairs it is worth remembering that opposites tend to attract and your initial enemies can be relatively easily brought on side. This happens because people don't expect kindness from a rival and when they receive it they are more drawn to that person overall than they are to a person they expect good treatment as a given all of the time. A person or group with whom you begin on a very amicable level can only be held satisfied with great difficulty.

> 'It pays to know the enemy — not least because at some time you may have the opportunity to turn him into a friend.' ~ Margaret Thatcher

> 'Acquaintance softens prejudices.' ~ Aesop, *The Fox and the Lion*

94. Listen to Customers More than Experts

The Turks then launched a surprise counterattack on Tafilah and the situation in the town turned to panic.

> "Dhiab the Sheikh had told us harrowing tales of the disaffection of the townspeople, to increase the splendour of his own loyalty; but my impression was that they were stout fellows of great potential use. To prove it I sat out on my roof, or walked in the dark up and down the steep alleys, cloaked against recognition, with my guards unobtrusively about me within call. So we heard what passed. The people were in a very passion of fear, nearly dangerous, abusing everybody and everything: but there was nothing pro-Turkish abroad. They were in horror of the Turks returning, ready to do all in their physical capacity to support against them a leader with fighting intention. This was satisfactory, for it chimed with my hankering to stand where we were and fight stiffly."

Lawrence doesn't accept the word of the town mayor at face value but instead goes out to hear what the real people on the ground are saying. Experts and technocrats often get paid to say or write things — which does not necessarily mean they are true. As mentioned in Lesson 15, marketing experts in large companies are paid to invent or imitate fancy concepts which they believe will resonate with consumers but the failure to go out and interact with a diverse range of people means they are always going to be somewhat distanced from reality in this respect.

Richard Branson is a great example of a CEO who is in touch with the man on the street. When he flies on his own airline he sits next to people in economy class and chats with them. He truly believes that the man on the street has more common sense than many big bosses. The opinions of people might be wrong but by taking a large sample you can use the crowd as a barometer of good sense, which will often get you closer to the mark than isolated conjecture. Crowds may not be incredibly innovative and they tend to follow each other, but on matters of fact they usually get it right. This was proven by the Victorian polymath Francis Galton, who in 1906 discovered that the average guesses of a group of 800 people managed to correctly estimate the weight of an ox, even though no individual got the number exactly right.

Intelligent people don't take so-called experts' word as gospel, especially in matters of marketing. They always double check the facts and are careful not to make sweeping conclusions based on small samples.

> 'Experts often possess more data than judgment. Elites can become so inbred that they produce haemophiliacs who bleed to death as soon as they are nicked by the real world.' ~ Colin Powell

95. Privately Challenge Established Doctrines

Having marshalled the battle and slain the Turks, Lawrence and his Arab fighters return to the village amid falling snow and freezing temperatures.

> "Next day and the next it snowed yet harder. We were weatherbound, and as the days passed in monotony we lost the hope of doing. We should have pushed past Kerak on the heels of victory, frighting the Turks to Amman with our rumour: as it was, nothing came of all the loss and effort, except a report which I sent over to the British headquarters in Palestine for the Staff's consumption. It was meanly written for effect, full of quaint smiles and mock simplicities; and made them think me a modest amateur, doing his best after the great models; not a clown, leering after them where they with Foch, bandmaster, at their head went drumming down the old road of effusion of blood into the house of Clausewitz. Like the battle, it was a nearly-proof parody of regulation use. Headquarters loved it, and innocently, to crown the jest, offered me a decoration on the strength of it. We should have more bright breasts in the Army if each man was able without witnesses, to write out his own despatch."

Lawrence has the courage to adopt a contrarian position. Healthy scepticism and radical ideas are the reason his war was a success. Lawrence was also pragmatic enough to recognise that he needed to dance to the tune of his superiors, who had the power to restrict his ability to conduct the campaign. Sometimes in an enterprise, the ends justify the means and this may require pulling the wool over the eyes of so-called superiors or opponents, or keeping people in the dark as to certain aspects of the operation, while not lying outright to anyone. Good leaders can do this because they are so convinced of their vision of reality and are so well-informed, that the value of their judgment is superior to that of any distant bystanders. He didn't ask for permission to fight in his irregular way and abandon the prevailing military dogma, because he knew it would not be granted. He knew that people are too conservative and dismissive of new ideas, even if they are founded in good sense.

'If it's a good idea, go ahead and do it. It is much easier to apologize than it is to get permission.' ~ Rear Admiral Grace Hopper

While Lawrence was playing a superior game, he reported to his superiors in Cairo by saying the things that they wished to hear. Initially he played down his strategy, intelligence and innovation in order to keep them compliant. Lawrence perfectly understood the principle that,

'The meaning of your communication is the response that you get.' ~ Richard Bandler & John Grinder, The Structure of Magic

96. Sometimes You Have to Get Out to Come Back In

Roughing out the utterly miserable January days, Lawrence strikes South in a soul crushing search for camp. He returns to Tafialh find that Faisal's brother Zeid has spent the gold that Lawrence had brought for the coming campaign.

> "I was aghast; for this meant the complete ruin of my plans and hopes, the collapse of our effort to keep faith with Allenby. Zeid stuck to his word that the money was all gone. Afterwards I went off to learn the truth from Nasir, who was in bed with fever. He despondently said that everything was wrong--Zeid too young and shy to counter his dishonest, cowardly counsellors.
>
> All night I thought over what could be done, but found a blank; and when morning came could only send word to Zeid that, if he would not return the money, I must go away. He sent me back his supposed account of the spent money. While we were packing, Joyce and Marshall arrived. They had ridden from Guweira to give me a pleasant surprise. I told them why it had happened that I was going back to Allenby to put my further employment in his hands. Joyce made a vain appeal to Zeid, and promised to explain to Feisal.
>
> He would close down my affairs and disperse my bodyguard. So I was able, with only four men, to set off, late that very afternoon, for Beersheba, the quickest way to British Headquarters. The coming of spring made the first part of the ride along the edge of the Araba scarp surpassingly beautiful, and my farewell mood showed me its beauties, keenly."

Failure is sometimes an opportunity to find a better path. To go to a higher authority and get a clean break from a negative situation rather than sitting and suffering.

It's important to know when to cut your losses so that you can come back stronger. Lawrence throws in his hand with minimal fuss and heartache. He simply makes haste and gets on with it as a realist and pragmatist.

Successful people know, often from bitter experience, that if you can't change something you either put up with it or you get out. There are only two ways to go. By following this philosophy you make life a lot easier on yourself and pursue the paths of least resistance to an ultimately successful conclusion.

97. Put Yourself in Others' Shoes

At Allenby's headquarters in Beersheba, Palestine, a conference convenes between the British Command.

> "At this Conference it was determined that the Arab Army move instantly to the Maan Plateau, to take Maan. That the British cross the Jordan, occupy Salt, and destroy south of Amman as much of the railway as possible; especially the great tunnel. It was debated what share the Amman Arabs should take in the British operation. Bols thought we should join in the advance. I opposed this, since the later retirement to Salt would cause rumour and reaction, and it would be easier if we did not enter till this had spent itself.
>
> Chetwode, who was to direct the advance, asked how his men were to distinguish friendly from hostile Arabs, since their tendency was a prejudice against all wearing skirts. I was sitting skirted in their midst and replied, naturally, that skirt-wearers disliked men in uniform. The laugh clinched the question, and it was agreed that we support the British retention of Salt only after they came to rest there."

Eliminating the possibility for misunderstanding between people of different cultures is a key part of international business. The British commander and his men didn't really trust the Arabs and Lawrence replies that the Arabs wouldn't trust them either. Therefore they decided on separating the two forces until the town was fully secure and the intensity of conditions for conflict abated.

Lack of cross cultural trust is a major hurdle in international business and has been the downfall of many a promising deal. One of the rules of cross cultural communication is to view the people of different cultures as being equals, not objects of curiosity, but human beings much the same as ourselves.

As the psychologist Elmar Holenstein points out in his *12 Rules for Avoiding Intercultural Misunderstandings*, humans suffer from the inclination to take things at face value and project and magnify our own shortcomings and fears in magnified form among members of other groups. We are generally too quick to pigeon-hole people and label whole groups with sweeping generalisations, when a bit of further enquiry would prove the simple truth that people are people.

The sooner we can understand that, just as Lawrence did in embracing the Arab culture, the sooner we can forge ahead as a real team, free from petty prejudices and misapprehensions regarding supposed flaws in national character.

Chapter IX

Lesson 98

Enfranchising People

The Ruin of High Hope — Précis

In the early spring of 1918, while preparing for the assault on the Turkish stronghold at Ma'an, some of the Arab officers had a change of heart with the British plan and decided not to support it. Nevertheless, Lawrence supervises the promised shipment of supplies for the Arab troops, still with the intention of linking up with the British when they had taken the city of Amman.

Just as the British broke through in Amman, they were counter attacked and pushed back into the Jordan Valley. The plan had failed. Lawrence returns to Faisal. On the way he discovers that the Arabs have taken the crest next to Ma'an and succeeded in smashing the train line beyond repair. On the third day, the French artillery run out of ammunition and the Arab infantry fail to take the main train station. The Turks were holding out.

Now it was the turn of the British under Dawnay to take the station with an intricately worked plan involving armoured cars, aircraft, systematic bridge bombing and co-ordinated advances. The Turks surrendered after a day of attack and bombardment. The next day, with most of the Arabs away, loaded with booty, the remaining force find Ramla station abandoned. By the third day, all the Arabs were gone and so were most of the Turks. They content themselves with blowing up more bridges and wrecking as much of the railway as possible along an eighty mile stretch encompassing several stations. Lawrence then returns to Allenby in Suez.

After the British setback in Amman, their resources and options were constrained. However, Lawrence manages to secure two thousand camels to mobilise the Arab force. This means a huge amount to the Arabs and Faisal is overjoyed at the news. Spirit in the Aqaba camp was buzzing as successes increased and preparations were made for a new push to finally capture Damascus. Lawrence advises Faisal to ask his father for reinforcements of regular troops. Meanwhile the British forces in Egypt receive reinforcements from India and Mesopotamia. This meant that an attack before September was becoming a reality.

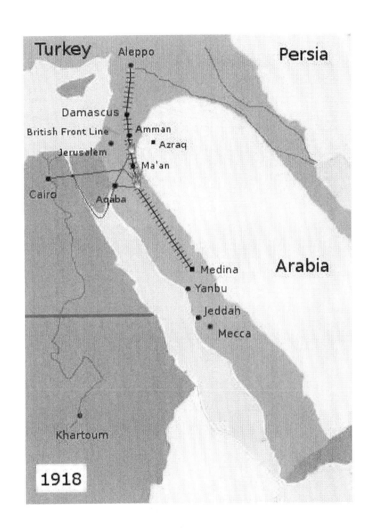

"In conjunction with Allenby we laid a triple plan to join hands across Jordan, to capture Maan, and to cut off Medina, in one operation. This was too proud and neither of us fulfilled his part. So the Arabs exchanged the care of the placid Medina railway for the greater burden of investing, in Moan, a Turk force as big as their available regular army.

To help in this duty Allenby increased our transport, that we might have longer range and more mobility. Moan was impregnable for us, so we concentrated on cutting its northern railway and diverting the Turkish effort to relieve its garrison from the Amman side.

Clearly no decision lay in such tactics: but the German advance in Flanders at this moment took from Allenby his British units; and consequently his advantage over the Turks. He notified us that he was unable to attack.

A stalemate, as we were, throughout 1918 was an intolerable prospect. We schemed to strengthen the Arab army for autumn operations near Deraa and in the Beni Sakhr country. If this drew off one division from the enemy in Palestine it would make possible a British ancillary attack, one of whose ends would be our junction in the lower Jordan valley, by Jericho. After a month's preparation this plan was dropped, because of its risk, and because a better offered."

Lesson 98

Enfranchising People

98. Treat People as Intelligent Individuals

Lawrence describes how the Arab Army differs from conventional military organisations in that they are largely irregular; without formal rules but possessing certain advantages.

"I was not discontented with this state of things, for it had seemed to me that discipline, or at least formal discipline, was a virtue of peace: a character or stamp by which to mark off soldiers from complete men, and obliterate the humanity of the individual. It resolved itself easiest into the restrictive, the making men not do this or that: and so could be fostered by a rule severe enough to make them despair of disobedience. It was a process of the mass, an element of the impersonal crowd, inapplicable to one man, since it involved obedience, a duality of will. It was not to impress upon men that their will must actively second the officer's, for then there would have been, as in the Arab Army and among irregulars, that momentary pause for thought transmission, or digestion; for the nerves to resolve the relaying private will into active consequence. On the contrary, each regular Army sedulously rooted out this significant pause from its companies on parade. The drill instructors tried to make obedience an instinct, a mental reflex, following as instantly on the command as though the motor power of the individual wills had been invested together in the system.

This was well, so far as it increased quickness: but it made no provision for casualties, beyond the weak assumption that each subordinate had his will-motor not atrophied, but reserved in perfect order, ready at the instant to take over his late superior's office; the efficiency of direction passing smoothly down the great hierarchy till vested in the senior of the two surviving privates.

It had the further weakness, seeing men's jealousy, of putting power in the hands of arbitrary old age, with its petulant activity: additionally corrupted by long habit of control, an indulgence which ruined its victim, by causing the death of his subjunctive mood. Also, it was an idiosyncrasy with me to distrust instinct, which had its roots in our animality. Reason seemed to give men something deliberately more precious than fear or pain: and this made me discount the value of peace smartness as a war-education."

Lawrence understands that it is better to use reason and have people be willing and voluntary in their behaviour than have to enforce things through rules and discipline.

Good companies try to eliminate bureaucracy and rules-for-rules'-sake. Power corrupts, so it's best if power is vested away from organisational bodies, departments and managers, and transferred to the individual to make his or her own decisions.

In niche industries which are knowledge intensive, the smaller player can afford to have a team of thinkers who are fairly independent to pursue their own good ideas. Niche businesses lead rather than follow and they truly focus on the customer. A smaller more human firm can split down the various market segments, enjoy increased dialogue with the customer and provide specialised products and services to suit people's real needs.

Like the lubbering Turks, big companies can't as easily engage in such vertical and horizontal disintegration. As we saw in Lesson 80, large entrenched firms inevitably become stagnant in their scope and their ability to inspire staff and customers, as well as being perennial latecomers in adopting new ways of doing things.

Chapter X

Lessons 99 — 110

Plans and Aspirations

Balancing for a Last Effort — Précis

In July 1918 Lawrence attends British preparations for the big push in September. In order to surprise the Turks, his mission was to persuade the Arabs not to attack, and delay them long enough in their current positions so as not to ruin Allenby's plans.

Lawrence and his fellow officers resolve on a raid by the British Camel Corps before the main British advance. During the early stage of the raid Lawrence is called back by Faisal and flies to Jafr for a conference of Arab sheiks. At this point in the narrative he goes into great depth regarding the nihilism and guilt he felt about deceiving the Arabs and promising their liberty.

When Lawrence returns, he hears that the British have taken the station garrison at Mudawwara with only four men killed. After this the British ask the Arabs to hold fast and not do anything rash until the whole push is effected. Lawrence then goes on to describe the political landscape at the time, mentioning the relationships between the Arabs and the Turks, that is, Faisal and Djemal Pasha and the correspondence between the two during the fighting. He also outlines what the British arrangements to all parties would be after the war, the Sykes-Picot Agreement between Britain and France and the beginning of legislated Zionism.

Next, Lawrence and a small group of British soldiers drive to the old base at Azraq Castle to plan the next raid. After another long journey through the desert in their armoured cars they finally link up with the Camel Corps. On the subsequent march to Amman the combined force of British and Arabs are spotted by a Turkish aeroplane. The Turks then turn out ready on the opposing clifftops and news comes that Turkish troops are also present in the villages below. Considerably outnumbered and encumbered, they decide to turn back via Azraq to the main camp at Aba al Lissan and plan their great thrust on the city of Daraa.

Later at camp, a political crisis erupts when Faisal's father in Mecca, King Hussein, becomes openly envious of Faisal's success and the decoration of Arab commanders by General Allenby in Cairo.

Lawrence, through his mercurial people skills and diplomacy finally manages to smooth everything over, avoiding widespread mutiny and disintegration of the revolt at this most crucial juncture.

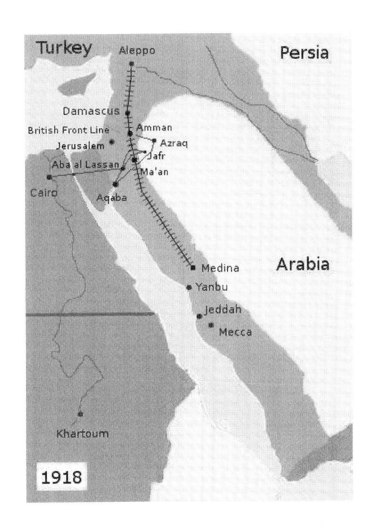

"Allenby, in rapid embodiment of reliefs from India and Mesopotamia, so surpassed hope that he was able to plan an autumn offensive. The near balance of the forces on each side meant that victory would depend on his subtly deceiving the Turks that their entire danger yet lay beyond the Jordan.

We might help, by lying quiet for six weeks, feigning a feebleness which should tempt the Turks to attack.

The Arabs were then to lead off at the critical moment by cutting the railway communications of Palestine.

Such bluff within bluff called for most accurate timing, since the balance would have been wrecked either by a premature Turkish retreat in Palestine, or by their premature attack against the Arabs beyond Jordan. We borrowed from Allenby some imperial camel corps to lend extra colour to our supposed critical situation; while preparations for Deraa went on with no more check than an untimely show of pique from King Hussein."

Lessons 99 — 110

Plans and Aspirations

99. Don't Be Dismayed by External Indifference

At GHQ in Cairo, the British generals scheme and debate possible lines of attack to finally finish the Turks.

"Weather and strengths might be matters of opinion: but Allenby meant to attack on September the nineteenth, and wanted us to lead off not more than four nor less than two days before he did. His words to me were that three men and a boy with pistols in front of Deraa on September the sixteenth would fill his conception; would be better than thousands a week before or a week after. The truth was, he cared nothing for our fighting power, and did not reckon us part of his tactical strength. Our purpose, to him, was moral, psychological, diathetic; to keep the enemy command intent upon the trans-Jordan front. In my English capacity I shared this view, but on my Arab side both agitation and battle seemed equally important, the one to serve the joint success, the other to establish Arab self-respect, without which victory would not be wholesome.

So, unhesitatingly, we laid the Young scheme aside and turned to build up our own. To reach Deraa from Aba el Lissan would take a fortnight: the cutting of the three railways and withdrawal to reform in the desert, another week. Our raiders must carry their maintenance for three weeks. The picture of what this meant was in my head – we had been doing it for two years – and so at once I gave Dawnay my estimate that our two thousand camels, in a single journey, without advanced depots or supplementary supply columns, would suffice five hundred regular mounted infantry, the battery of French quick-firing "point 65" mountain guns, proportionate machine-guns, two armoured cars, sappers, camel-scouts, and two aeroplanes until we had fulfilled our mission. This seemed like a liberal reading of Allenby's three men and a boy. We told Bartholomew, and received G.H.Q. Blessing."

Everyone has opinions but that doesn't mean they are right. If so-to-be-believed experts are negative towards your cause, don't pay too much heed. It is more realistic to be positive and self-actualising in your aims however doubtful outsiders may be.

One of the biggest problems in this world is that most people can't recognise talent. The default position for many is that of a doubting Thomas, only respecting something if they can see it already proven in the flesh.

The superior leader knows his business inside out and stays ahead of the bell curve. This means they can safely ignore negativity by visualising goals so clearly and articulating that vision so clearly that to them, the future is already a reality. The best leaders have faith in their own ideas and they don't give up on them. This was understood all too well by Lawrence who wrote, in his most famous line from *Seven Pillars:*

> *"All men dream: but not equally. Those who dream by night in the dusty recesses of their minds wake in the day to find that it was vanity: but the dreamers of the day are dangerous men, for they may act their dreams with open eyes, to make it possible."*

100. Don't Be Weighed Down by Convention in Lieu of True Understanding

Lawrence introduces the revised plan to the new British officer in the Arab camp, who stubbornly resists the idea.

"For Young's transport troubles I had little sympathy. He, a new comer, said my problems were insoluble: but I had done such things casually, without half his ability and concentration; and knew they were not even difficult. For the Camel Corps, we left him to grapple with weights and time-tables, since the British Army was his profession; and though he would not promise anything (except that it could not be done), done of course it was, and two or three days before the necessary time. The Deera raid was a different proposition, and point by point I disputed his conception of its nature and equipment.

I crossed out forage, the heaviest item, after Bair. Young became ironic upon the patient endurance of camels: but this year the pasture was grand in the Azrak Deraa region. From the men's food I cut off provision for the second attack, and the return journey. Young supposed aloud that the men would fight well hungry. I explained that we would live on the country. Young thought it a poor country to live on. I called it very good.

He said that the ten days' march home after the attacks would be a long fast: but I had no intention of coming back to Akaba. Then might he ask if it was defeat or victory which was in my mind? I pointed out how each man had a camel under him, and if we killed only six camels a day the whole force would feed abundantly. Yet this did not solace him. I went on to cut down his petrol, cars, ammunition, and everything else to the exact point, without margin, which would meet what we planned. In riposte he became aggressively regular. I prosed forth on my hoary theorem that we lived by our raggedness and beat the Turk by our uncertainty. Young's scheme was faulty, because precise."

The battleground of ideas is as important as the real battleground itself. Lawrence has a strong strategy backed up with deeper experience and he forces his argument through with logic.

People limit themselves by traditional approaches and what they conceive as proper ways of doing things when in fact they become encumbered by them. A conservative view is natural for people who have been incumbent and away from the firing line — the reality itself, for too long.

As mentioned in Lessons 15 and 94, a lot of corporate workers suffer from ivory tower syndrome and fail to connect and communicate daily with the real customers. By increments they become detached from the essence of the business, see risks in everything new and block ideas. Good leaders keep people raw and keep their feet firmly on the ground. Good leaders steel their organisations against not-invented-here syndrome and hidebound attitudes.

101. Ambition May Not Get You There, But It Will Get You Close

Spirits gradually rise within the camp at Aba al Lissan as the prospect of victory and glory in the coming assault capture the men's ambitions.

> "Our own family rifts were distressing, but inevitable. The Arab affair had now outgrown our rough and ready help-organization. But the next was probably the last act, and by a little patience we might make our present resources serve. The troubles were only between ourselves, and thanks to the magnificent unselfishness of Joyce, we preserved enough of team-spirit to prevent a complete breakdown, however high-handed I appeared: and I had a reserve of confidence to carry the whole thing, if need be, on my shoulders. They used to think me boastful when I said so: but my confidence was not so much ability to do a thing perfectly, as a preference for botching it somehow rather than letting it go altogether by default."

Lawrence is prepared to wing it if all else fails. People think 'winging it' is negligent, but as long as you really believe in something it's ok to make it up as you go along. You have more fun that way and you discover insights experientially — things that experts could never tell you because usually they haven't tried and failed, certainly not here-and-now; where you are. Winging it does not mean being underprepared or foolish. It means being determined and practical. What you lack in knowledge you can make up for with enthusiasm.

Having the confidence to attempt great things is a trait of great leaders and great companies. Even if your plan or part of your plan fails, rather than give up on the whole attempt you can always engage in damage limitation and a botched success that lets you learn and live to fight another day is far better than no success at all.

Having goals does not mean you will hit them exactly on schedule, but people who have goals usually get near enough and learn a lot in the process, while those who shy away from daring exploits never move forward.

102. Dress Well

At the conference of Sheiks in Jafr, Lawrence distinguishes himself through his demeanour and appearance.

> "Beside me sat Rahail, peacocking his lusty self in strident clothes. Under cover of the conversation he whispered me the name of each chief. They had not to ask who I was, for my clothes and appearance were peculiar in the desert. It was notoriety to be the only cleanshaven one, and I doubled it by wearing always the suspect pure silk, of the whitest (at least outside), with a gold and crimson Meccan head-rope, and gold dagger. By so dressing I staked a claim which Feisal's public consideration of me confirmed."

It is an old but true saying that 'the clothes maketh the man'. A manager should encourage the very best standards from his staff and lead by example to demonstrate pride, worthiness and urbanity.

Good workers dress for the job they want, not the job they have. They do this because they understand that impressions count. It's not fair that first impressions count but the fact is that they do and so being aware of this means people make positive assumptions about you.

103. Less Is More

During the conference, Faisal and Lawrence have to use all the craft in their power to sell the war to the Sheiks.

> "Many times in such councils had Feisal won over and set aflame new tribes, many times had the work fallen to me; but never until to-day had we been actively together in one company, reinforcing and relaying one another, from our opposite poles: and the work went like child's play; the Rualla melted in our double heat. We could move them with a touch and a word. There was tenseness, a holding of breath, the glitter of belief in their thin eyes so fixed on us.
>
> Feisal brought nationality to their minds in a phrase, which set them thinking of Arab history and language; then he dropped into silence for a moment: for with these illiterate masters of the tongue words were lively, and they liked to savour each, unmingled, on the palate. Another phrase showed them the spirit of Feisal, their fellow and leader, sacrificing everything for the national freedom; and then silence again, while they imagined him day and night in his tent, teaching, preaching, ordering and making friends: and they felt something of the idea behind this pictured man sitting there iconically, drained of desires, ambitions, weakness, faults; so rich a personality enslaved by an abstraction, made one-eyed, one armed, with the one sense and purpose, to live or die in its service."

With great integrity Faisal and Lawrence use simple soundbites, making emotional shortcuts so people can infer meanings for themselves without extended narrative and explicit explanation or exhortation. Pithy, short phrases can do more work than overstressed verbose talk which can seem desperate and boring. Brevity is the soul of wit and constraining yourself within short phrases of seven words or less is a golden rule for effective presenting. Key phrases don't have to be glib but they do need to provide a springboard for further storytelling and deeper insights.

'Simplicity is the ultimate sophistication.' ~ Leonardo da Vinci

104. Play On the Subconscious When Communicating

The two protagonists were not averse to using all the psychological techniques in their armoury to create the intended effect.

> "Our conversation was cunningly directed to light trains of their buried thoughts; that the excitement might be their own and the conclusions native, not inserted by us. Soon we felt them kindle: we leaned back, watching them move and speak, and vivify each other with mutual heat, till the air was vibrant, and in stammered phrases they experienced the first heave and thrust of notions which ran up beyond their sight. They turned to hurry us, themselves the begetters, and we laggard strangers: strove to make us comprehend the full intensity of their belief; forgot us; flashed out the means and end of our desire. A new tribe was added to our comity: though Nuri's plain 'Yes' at the end carried more than all had said."

This approach is linked to Lawrence's technique in Lesson 65 of using hidden commands and the Milton Model of hypnosis. Through subtle implication Faisal and Lawrence allow people to construct their own interpretations. Compliance comes best from persuasion, not power, and sometimes you don't have to push too hard to bring people around to your way of thinking. As such, a very effective method of selling is to feign disinterest in the product or topic at hand. It makes the other person sit up and think for themselves on the basis of your obvious logic and quiet self assurance.*

Uniting the tribes to fight in the Arab Revolt is a deeply emotional argument that Faisal and Lawrence are waging and so they can afford to be extremely subtle in their pitch. The subconscious mind is far more powerful than the conscious and thus they prefer to play on the deeper meanings without going to extra lengths to elucidate verbally.

> 'Don't turn your mind into an ammunition wagon, but turn it into a rifle to fire off other people's ammunition.' ~ Winston Churchill

The psychologist Albert Mehrabian famously discovered that when people talk about their feelings or attitudes, their facial expressions, body language, appearance and tone of voice can provide a lot more meaning than the actual words they say. Responding to emotions is far more deeply hard-wired in our evolutionary makeup than the ability to speak a language. Therefore when emotions are at stake, it is the implicit non-verbal meaning we register subconsciously which often carries more weight.

The best communicators are aware of the deeper connotations and contexts present in our interactions. They understand that the meaning of a message is the response that you get, and so they craft the unwritten content that lies between the lines as much as the actual words on the surface.

* Ironically, feigning disinterest works equally well when buying too. This is because when the roles are reversed it represents a conscious signal that gives the seller less power over the price and terms, and gives you more breathing space to negotiate.

105. People Are Not Rational

Despite being extremely convincing and effective, deep down Lawrence was not comfortable in his role.

> "For naturally I could not long deceive myself; but my part was worked out so flippantly that none but Joyce, Nesib and Mohammed el Dheilan seemed to know I was acting. With man-instinctive, anything believed by two or three had a miraculous sanction to which individual ease and life might honestly be sacrificed. To man-rational, wars of nationality were as much a cheat as religious wars, and nothing was worth fighting for: nor could fighting, the act of fighting, hold any need of intrinsic virtue. Life was so deliberately private that no circumstances could justify one man in laying violent hands upon another's: though a man's own death was his last free will, a saving grace and measure of intolerable pain."

Lawrence highlights the discrepancy between the rationality and instinct in human society, by suggesting that 'man-rational' would never involve himself in something as absurd as war. But the sad truth that Lawrence was fully aware of was that humans as a whole are not rational creatures. Instead we are very much the 'man-instinctive' he describes; following blindly and absolutely convinced in the need for doing so.

Edward Bernays was a nephew of Sigmund Freud and probably the most powerful social manipulator in modern history. Bernays was the first public relations king. In fact he invented the concept by understanding that companies needed to engage the general populace in order to create a positive image of their products. On behalf of big corporations like cigarette firms and car makers, Bernays instigated subtle yet widespread propaganda stunts and campaigns which subconsciously linked goods to images of a desirable consumerist lifestyle. These in turn propagated America's capitalist system at a time when it was under threat from the spread of a competing ideology in the form of communism. Bernays was successful in changing people's attitudes because he understood that human beings are emotional rather than rational creatures. That is, we are motivated by emotional impulses more than logical ones.

It is a simple fact of human nature that we form gregarious societies based on attraction. People naturally follow and we value the opinion of others. That's why name dropping, fads and groupthink work no matter how ridiculous they may be. We all want to feel part of a group. We are attracted to each other by metaphysical emotional energy. Just as the physical universe is based on attraction, so is life. This is what entrepreneurs have to harness. People like Steve Jobs knew all too well that if you can create a truly unique and ground breaking product, people will buy into your whole philosophy as long as it benefits their life and especially their status. Jobs tuned himself into the needs and desires of 'man-instinctive' and as a result, he created one of the world's most profitable businesses.

106. Go Beyond the Material Goal

Lawrence ruminates on his preaching, and struggles to justify his moulding of the minds of the Arabs.

> "We made the Arabs strain on tip-toe to reach our creed, for it led to works, a dangerous country where men might take the deed for the will. My fault, my blindness of leadership (eager to find a quick means to conversion) allowed them this finite image of our end, which properly existed only in unending effort towards unattainable imagined light. Our crowd seeking light in things were like pathetic dogs snuffling round the shank of a lamp-post. It was only myself who valeted the abstract, whose duty took him beyond the shrine."

The fact that Lawrence is of a different ethnicity to the Arabs is irrelevant because he is preaching not just an inter-ethnic war but a higher ideology of liberation and self-determination on an international rather than local scale.

Human beings are attracted to each other firstly on the basis of a common language, but secondly on religion and ideology. Social experiments have shown that even non-religious people of diverse ethnicities will congregate on the basis of religion, ideology and class. Ethnicity, being part of the physical rather than the metaphysical world, comes a distant third when it comes to uniting people.

Lawrence knew that ideas and dreams are bigger drivers of will than concrete objects like money. Leaders have to challenge people and articulate a more intangible goal that is greater than simple monetary values. If something is too easy, too common or too obvious, people don't fire themselves up about it. Scarcity, measured-difficultly and a certain amount of unpredictability, motivate people.

> 'There are only two forces in the world, the sword and the spirit. In the long run the sword will always be conquered by the spirit.' ~ Napoleon

107. What You Think You Will Become, You Will Become

Wondering why he was flung into this predicament, he concludes that he must have wanted it. . .

> "The irony was in my loving objects before life or ideas; the incongruity in my answering the infectious call of action, which laid weight on the diversity of things. It was a hard task for me to straddle feeling and action. I had had one craving all my life--for the power of self-expression in some imaginative form--but had been too diffuse ever to acquire a technique. At last accident, with perverted humour, in casting me as a man of action had given me place in the Arab Revolt, a theme ready and epic to a direct eye and hand, thus offering me an outlet in literature, the technique-less art. Whereupon I became excited only over mechanism. The epic mode was alien to me, as to my generation. Memory gave me no clue to the heroic, so that I could not feel such men as Auda in myself. He seemed fantastic as the hills of Rumm, old as Mallory."

Deep down Lawrence always wanted to be a writer and now the opportunity presented itself perfectly to him — not just be a writer but to be a writer of an epic, continuing in the tradition of some of history's greatest leaders.

Often in life, the opportunities you seek will present themselves coincidentally, but you need to recognise that chance when it presents itself. If you constantly take random avenues in daily life, you will guide yourself towards the mastery of new things in your own style. Subconsciously you walk towards a reality which you have envisioned for yourself and the synchronicities and coincidences which seem divinely presented are there to be seized. All you have to do is keep on going.

> 'It is no great wonder if in long process of time, while fortune takes her course hither and thither, numerous coincidences should spontaneously occur.' ~ Plutarch

'The soul attracts that which it secretly harbours, that which it loves, and also that which it fears. It reaches the height of its cherished aspirations. It falls to the level of its unchastened desires – and circumstances are the means by which the soul receives its own.' ~ James Allen, *As A Man Thinketh* (1903)

'Once you make a decision, the universe conspires to make it happen.' ~ Ralph Waldo Emerson

108. Attack the Leadership

Lawrence reveals that Faisal has been surreptitiously weakening the enemy by keeping a secret correspondence with the Turkish leader, Djemal Pasha.

"True, that accommodation with Jemal was not possible. He had lopped the tall heads of Syria, and we should deny our friends' blood if we admitted him to our peace: but by indicating this subtly in our reply we might widen the national-clerical rift in Turkey.

Our particular targets were the anti-German section of the General Staff, under Mustapha Kemal, who were too keen on the 'Turkishness' of their mission to deny the right of autonomy to the Arabic provinces of the Ottoman Empire. Accordingly, Feisal sent back tendencious answers; and the correspondence continued brilliantly. The Turkish soldiers began to complain of the pietists, who put relics before strategy. The Nationalists wrote that Feisal was only putting into premature and disastrous activity their own convictions upon the just, inevitable self-determination of Turkey.

Knowledge of the ferment affected Jemal's determination. At first we were offered autonomy for Hejaz. Then Syria was admitted to the benefit: then Mesopotamia. Feisal seemed still not content; so Jemal's deputy (while his master was in Constantinople) boldly added a Crown to the offered share of Hussein of Mecca. Lastly, they told us they saw logic in the claim of the prophet's family to the spiritual leadership of Islam!

The comic side of the letters must not obscure their real help in dividing the Turkish Staff. Old-fashioned Moslems thought the Sherif an unpardonable sinner. Modernists thought him a sincere but impatient Nationalist misled by British promises. They had a desire to correct him rather by argument than by military defeat.

Their strongest card was the Sykes-Picot agreement, an old-style division of Turkey between England, France, and Russia, made public by the Soviets. Jemal read the more spiteful paragraphs at a banquet in Beyrout. For a while the disclosure hurt us; justly, for we and the French had thought to plaster over a split in policy by a formula vague enough for each to interpret in his divergent way."

The Sykes-Picot Agreement was a secret treaty to divide up the Middle East between Britain and France after the collapse of the Ottoman Empire at the end of World War 1. The document was leaked by the Russians and *The Guardian* newspaper, so that both the Arabs and the Turks discovered that the Allies were plotting to at best ignore them and at worst rule over them after the conclusion of the war. Meanwhile, Lawrence and Faisal were secretly seeking to instigate divisions at the very top of the Turkish regime, just as the British and French were secretly trying to divide the whole region.

By creating divisions you keep the opposition weak. If you befriend one half of the leadership and attack the other half, then that disharmony trickles down to the rank and file with far more ease than attacking from the bottom up. This is also true when marketing a product. If you take aim at, or associate yourself with, the most influential players in the industry, people will notice you.

> 'How do you attack an organisation? You attack its Leadership.' ~ Julian Assange

> 'Defeat the enemy by capturing their chief.' ~ *The Thirty-Six Stratagems*

109. Develop a Wide Thirst for Learning

On his thirtieth birthday at Bair on the eve of the great Anglo-Arab march to Amman, Lawrence engages in some deep reflection on his personality and the path he has chosen.

> "I quickly outgrew ideas. So I distrusted experts, who were often intelligences confined within high walls, knowing indeed every paving-stone of their prison courts: while I might know from what quarry the stones were hewn and what wages the mason earned. I gainsaid them out of carelessness, for I had found materials always apt to serve a purpose, and Will a sure guide to some one of the many roads leading from purpose to achievement. There was no flesh. Many things I had picked up, dallied with, regarded, and laid down; for the conviction of doing was not in me. Fiction seemed more solid than activity. Self-seeking ambitions visited me, but not to stay, since my critical self would make me fastidiously reject their fruits. Always I grew to dominate those things into which I had drifted, but in none of them did I voluntarily engage. Indeed, I saw myself a danger to ordinary men, with such capacity yawing rudderless at their disposal."

Lawrence is a polymathic autodidact, constantly searching for new ideas and new areas for growth. He is ready to study and learn the details and intricacies concerning things that other people overlook. Lawrence knows his history and has the marvellous ability to see its relevance in the present. He recognises the value of lessons learnt from the past, including from the Crusades, which deeply inspired him. His curiosity and intellect know no boundaries and he wishes to master those disciplines and practices with which he comes into contact. Lawrence knows that he is not as experienced as other generals and he understands that he is something of a novice. But he is not afraid to learn on his own accord, challenge established ideas and put into action new ways of doing things. He embodies the spirit of eclecticism that Confucius describes when he said:

> 'Acquire new knowledge whilst thinking over the old, and you may become a teacher of others.'

110. Leadership Is More About Character than Brains

While Lawrence thought himself a failure, he had great admiration for his commander-in-chief.

> "There were qualities like courage which could not stand alone, but must be mixed with a good or bad medium to appear. Greatness in Allenby showed itself other, in category: self-sufficient, a facet of character, not of intellect. It made superfluous in him ordinary qualities; intelligence, imagination, acuteness, industry, looked silly beside him. He was not to be judged by our standards, any more than the sharpness of bow of a liner was to be judged by the sharpness of razors. He dispensed with them by his inner power."

Lawrence idolised Allenby for his redoubtable personal qualities. A similar figure of note was Horatio Nelson, Britain's greatest and bravest hero. Nelson's sheer force of character set him apart from other, more intelligent, wealthier and more orthodox leaders. People with strong characters are not scared of being different and are not afraid of breaking the mould with original thinking.

> 'Eccentricity has always abounded when and where strength of character had abounded; and the amount of eccentricity in a society has generally been proportional to the amount of genius, mental vigour, and courage which it contained.' ~ John Stuart Mill

The British educational system has traditionally emphasised the shaping of a child's character over the need to teach subject matter. In the 18th century, Voltaire remarked on the difference between this type of moral education and the continental style. And it is still true today that outside in the real world, a knowledge of facts or an ability to do calculus is not going to take you half as far as interpersonal charm and generally friendly or gentlemanly social skills. It is the ability to relate to others, not an ability to recite knowledge, which is important in business. Ultimately it is the emotional virtues of a person which are greater than the intellectual virtues, in motivating and gaining trust from people.

Chapter XI

Lessons 111 — 120

Personal Growth

The House is Perfected — Précis

The campaign is reaching its end game. The buoyant and diverse streams of Arab and British forces gather at Azraq in early September ready to take the town of Daraa from where they will make the last push for Damascus.

On the first day of the march, a British bomber gets into a fight with a Turkish patrol plane and the enemy aircraft is shot down in flames to the delight of the watching army. The next day, Lawrence and a gang of men sally out in two armoured cars to blow the railway line and a nearby bridge while the army march on and a squadron of bombers smash Daraa for the first time. The destruction of the bridge means that the Turks are stranded from reinforcements. Shortly after this, the whole area is taken by the Arabs. With Allenby's British advance through Palestine about to begin, victory was now almost completely secured.

While blowing the railway and being bombed from the air, Lawrence and his men move on more bridges, stations and towns along the line. At each station the Turks duly surrender, their stores are plundered and the telegraph cut. Throughout this, their numbers swell with peasants from the surrounding villages joining the movement.

At one village a strong guard of Turkish soldiers hold the bridge that Lawrence had previously tried and failed to destroy. The Captain secretly defects to the Arabs and they make a plan to ambush the station with his help. However, the plan is called off as the Captain is arrested and a train of German and Turkish reinforcements arrives to put the situation in order. Lawrence then resolves to fly to Allenby and secure aeroplanes and money; to stop the Turks incessant bombing and monitoring of their movements, and settle dissatisfaction in the bombed villages. Meanwhile in Azraq following a raid on a Turkish post, they hear the news that Allenby has smashed through and routed the Turks in Palestine. It was now going to be a race to Damascus.

As soon as Lawrence returns with two Bristol Fighters, more enemy aircraft loom into sight. The British planes are scrambled and shoot down two German biplanes. The Handley-Page, a magnificent machine and the pride of the RAF, was also sent over from Egypt. It was now determined that Damascus could be seized in a week. The Arab Army now numbered in the tens of thousands and the enemy had fairly disintegrated in panic. In Tafas, the Arabs discover the town population completely massacred. They chase down the retreating column and reap vengeance. The Arab rampage goes into overdrive and the Turkish army are cut to pieces in a hopeless retreat.

At the same moment, the war in Europe was also drawing to a conclusion. Lawrence and the Arabs had thrown off a five hundred-year empire and fairly and squarely beaten the British into Damascus. The victorious army were cheered through the streets and Faisal was fully installed as King of the Arabs.

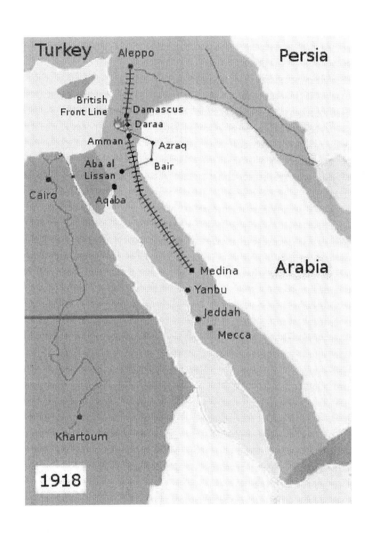

"Our mobile column of aeroplanes, armoured cars, Arab regulars and Beduin collected at Azrak, to cut the three railways out of Deraa. The southern line we cut near Mafrak; the northern at Arar; the western by Mezerib. We circumnavigated Deraa, and rallied, despite air raids, in the desert.

Next day Allenby attacked, and in a few hours had scattered the Turkish armies beyond recovery.

I flew to Palestine for aeroplane help, and got orders for a second phase of the thrust northward.

We moved behind Deraa to hasten its abandonment. General Barrow joined us; in his company we advanced to Kiswe, and there met the Australian Mounted corps. Our united forces entered Damascus unopposed. Some confusion manifested itself in the city. We strove to allay it; Allenby arrived and smoothed out all difficulties. Afterwards he let me go."

Lessons 111 — 120

Personal Growth

111. Stay One Step Ahead of the Pack

Driving through the desert in the comfort of a Rolls Royce, on the way to Azraq, the British officers stop at Bair to learn from the concerned Arabs that the Turks have counter-attacked.

> "At Bair we heard from the alarmed Beni Sakhr that the Turks, on the preceding day, had launched suddenly westward from Hesa into Tafileh. Mifleh thought I was mad, or most untimely merry, when I laughed outright at the news which four days sooner would have held up the Azrak expedition: but, now we were started, the enemy might take Aba el Lissan, Guweira, Akaba itself – and welcome! Our formidable talk of advance by Amman had pulled their leg nearly out of socket, and the innocents were out to counter our feint. Each man they sent south was a man, or rather ten men, lost."

The Turks are behind the curve on the Arab strategy and mode of warfare. The Arabs are easily able to wrong foot them and drive in the opposite direction. In work and business it's often a good strategy to allow competitors to be contented with the low-hanging fruit. That's what the passive majority do but it's amazing how a little extra effort and planning can set you far apart from mediocrity. You don't have to ostentatiously promote yourself but you can be surreptitiously working towards a higher goal, a better market segment or developing a superior product safe in your vision for the future.

> 'A military operation involves deception. Even though you are competent, appear incompetent. Though effective, appear ineffective.' ~ Sun-zi

We all need the courage to take the opposite path from the crowd sometimes even if that involves ridicule. In parts of this book I mention the importance of the group and the wisdom of the crowd but of course there is an antithesis to this. Successful individuals view their public behaviour and interactions as a business person would rather than from the perspective of a cool kid who wants to be popular. This demonstrates learning, conviction and maturity. Such an attitude of professional integrity secures your long term reputation as a force to be reckoned with in the market place.

112. Keep Flexible

While resting in camp at Azraq before the push on Daraa, Lawrence, with victory finally within reach, is imbued with a sense of serenity and assuredness.

> "Long after, I heard that Winterton rose each dawn and examined the horizon, lest my carelessness subject us to surprise: and at Umtaiye and Sheikh Saad the British for days thought we were a forlorn hope. Actually I knew (and surely said?) that we were as safe as anyone in the world at war. Because of the pride they had, I never saw their doubt of my plans.
>
> These plans were a feint against Amman and a real cutting of the Deraa railways: further than this we hardly went, for it was ever my habit, while studying alternatives, to keep the stages in solution.
>
> The public often gave credit to Generals because it had seen only the orders and the result: even Foch said (before he commanded troops) that Generals won battles: but no General ever truly thought so. The Syrian campaign of September 1918 was perhaps the most scientifically perfect in English history, one in which force did least and brain most. All the world, and especially those who served them, gave the credit of the victory to Allenby and Bartholomew: but those two would never see it in our light, knowing how their inchoate ideas were discovered in application, and how their men, often not knowing, wrought them."

In war and in business, as soon as the battle begins, the plan must change. If you are fighting a campaign, you need a solid end-goal in mind but at the same time you must be prepared for unexpected things to happen and realise that unexpected things will happen. In life, business, sport and war, plans don't always come off and thus we need other options to fall back on and further avenues to go down.

Cybernetics is the study of systems — be they biological, computerised or social. In 1956 the Scottish cyberneticist, Ross Ashby, who was very much the father of the field, coined his 'Law of Requisite Variety' which states that: *only variety absorbs variety*.

If we look at nature as a system of living things interacting with each other, the organism which is most able to adapt — to vary its behaviour — is the organism which is most likely to control that system. In such systems, over-specialisation in the bigger scheme of things is detrimental because when a big change suddenly occurs, the company or person or culture which is least able to vary its behaviour is usually the one which will become irrelevant. Likewise in work and life, the person with the most choices available to them is the person most likely to succeed in any given situation.

Lack of requisite variety is why ancient civilisations died away. A culture becomes so powerful and stable that it cannot recognise, never mind embrace, the need for change. This in turn breeds traditionalist instincts, conservatism and restrictions of freedom. When the outside world changed in a big way, glorious old civilisations like the Ottoman Empire were unable to move positively against the new order of things.

One thing we can learn from history is that the more open a culture is to change, the more chance it has of surviving. This truth can be applied to many aspects of society. When the government introduces regulations to curb derivatives trading in the City, bankers find a way around the laws to stay one step ahead of the authorities, who then have to respond with even tighter laws. This ongoing cycle of competition reflects itself in everything from traffic congestion to natural selection and political organisation.

Therefore a leader in pursuit of a goal should act like a rhino regarding strategy but a fox in his real-time tactical approach, adjusting flexibly to changing market conditions. In the same vein, a healthy company is a decentralised one that constantly innovates, toys with new ideas and searches out areas for growth.

'All things are ready if our minds be so.' ~ Shakespeare, *Henry V*

113. If You Ask People Not to Do Something, They Will Want to Do It

Such a small force occupying Azraq, so close to the enemy in Amman, looked to be a risky position. However, they had an armoured car, a good vantage point and could rely on manipulating the tribes between themselves and the line to keep the small Turkish post feeling threatened, while the real target was much further north at Daraa.

> "By our establishment at Azrak the first part of our plan, the feint, was accomplished. We had sent our 'horsemen of St. George', gold sovereigns, by the thousand to the Beni Shakr, purchasing all the barley on their threshing floors: begging them not to mention it, but we would require it for our animals and for our British allies, in a fortnight. Dhiab of Tafileh – that jerky, incomplete hobbledehoy – gossiped the news instantly through to Kerak."

Reverse psychology and negative suggestion, especially repeated suggestion, can be very useful ploys in management, marketing, sales and negotiation. The subconscious mind does not process negative syntax, so inserting 'no', 'don't', 'not', 'can't' etc. into a phrase helps to surreptitiously plant a seed in a person's mind, which will remain for longer than the specific but semantically light function words around it. Added to this is desire. If you want to disseminate information, you tell people not to tell anyone. If you want a customer to desire your product, you suggest that it's difficult for you to give it to them. It's human nature to take forbidden fruit, just as if you show people a big bright red button and tell them not to press it, they inevitably will.

As elucidated by the legendary investor Charlie Munger, the "lollapalooza effect"* is the common situation whereby the effect of suggestions is amplified by the emotional state of the subjects involved. The men first create excitement by turning up laden with gold, ready to purchase a huge quantity of food. This sparks a fever of commercial and social energy among the locals. Therefore before applying suggestive commands, the more you can stimulate the emotions of the person, the more effective your command will be.

* See: *The Psychology of Human Misjudgement*, talk at Harvard University (1995).

114. Seize the Initiative

Two days later, the Arab Army manage to capture and rip up the railway line below Darra, cutting off Amman, Ma'an and southern Palestine from Turkish control.

> "Young and I cut the telegraph, here an important network of trunk and local lines, indeed the Palestine army's main link with their homeland. It was pleasant to imagine Linan von Sandars' fresh curse, in Nazareth, as each severed wire tanged back from the clippers. We did them slowly, with ceremony, to draw out the indignation. The Turks' hopeless lack of initiative made their army a 'directed' one, so that by destroying the telegraphs we went far towards turning them into a leaderless mob. After the telegraph we blew in the points, and planted tulips: not very many, but enough to annoy. While we worked a light engine came down the line from Deraa on patrol. The bang and dust-clouds of our tulips perturbed it. It withdrew discreetly. Later an aeroplane visited us."

Big organisations tend to look inwards instead of outwards and thus they are slow to react. Often management are so disconnected from their staff that they become the inert 'leaderless mob' Lawrence describes. So many people in big organisations just do what they are told to and don't really respond to what is happening in the market. All of which means that it is very easy for a smaller more vibrant player to run rings around the established competition.

This is a straightforward strategy as long as the entrepreneur takes the time to empower people to think outside of traditional organisational boundaries to the real world where the market and customers exist. The prototypical management guru Peter Drucker, illustrates this point in his seminal book *The Effective Executive* (1967),

> 'Every executive, whether his organization is a business or a research laboratory, a government agency, a large university or the air force, sees the inside — the organization — as close and immediate reality. He sees the outside only through thick and distorting lenses, if at all. What goes on outside is usually not even

known first-hand. It is received through an organizational filter of reports, that is, in an already predigested and highly abstract form that imposes organizational criteria of relevance on the outside reality.

The fewer people, the smaller, the less activity inside, the more nearly perfect is the organization in terms of its only reason for existence: the service to the environment.

This outside, this environment which is the true reality, is well beyond effective control from the inside. But it is the inside of the organization that is most visible to the executive. It is the inside that has immediacy for him. Its relations and contacts, its problems and challenges, its crosscurrents and gossip reach him and touch him at every point. Unless he makes special efforts to gain direct access to outside reality, he will become increasingly inside-focussed. The higher up in the organization he goes, the more will his attention be drawn to problems and challenges of the inside rather than to events on the outside.'

115. Collect Information Voraciously

Having plundered an abandoned Turkish station, the men rest for food while streams of peasants arrive from the surrounding villages.

> "Visitors were our eyes, and had to be welcomed. My business was to see every one with news, and let him talk himself out to me, afterwards arranging and combining the truth of these points into a complete picture in my mind. Complete, because it gave me certainty of judgement: but it was not conscious nor logical, for my informants were so many that they informed me to distraction, and my single mind bent under all its claims."

Two heads are better than one and ten heads are better than two heads. The circle of people that you know are a huge untapped resource. One of the traits of good leaders is that they constantly utilise the people around them as a sounding board for ideas and decisions. They collect opinions on the basis of quantity, not quality.

It doesn't harm to ask a question that you already know the answer to, or you *think* you know the answer to. Even if you are convinced as to the truth of your own viewpoint, getting further opinions, good or bad, right or wrong, at worst affirms what you already know, in the main gives you slightly finer understanding of the situation, and at best it may provide a revelation. Constantly questioning and listening to people is a healthy practice even if people say things you don't like to hear or things which are completely untrue. The key is in surrounding yourself with intelligent people and not relying on too small a sample.

Machiavelli best illustrated that good leaders cultivate a circle of trusted advisors whom they allow to speak honestly, but only when asked. As such, leaders should show their anger not when they hear bad news, but when they feel people are not being totally honest. Bad leaders on the other hand are egotistical. They don't like to be upset or disagreed with and they install yes-men and sycophants who fawn and tiptoe around them, perhaps eventually plotting to usurp them. The first of these archetype leaders is grounded in reality and the actual demands of the environment, the other is based on distrust and intellectual dishonesty.

116. Don't Compromise on the Really Important Things

As people flock into the camp, Lawrence finds their presence and the revolt's sudden popularity unnerving.

> "Men came pouring down from the north on horse, on camel, and on foot, hundreds and hundreds of them in a terrible grandeur of enthusiasm, thinking this was the final occupation of the country, and that Nasir would seal his victory by taking Deraa in the night Even the magistrates of Deraa came to open us their town. By acceding we should hold the water supply of the railway station, which must inevitably yield: yet later, if the ruin of the Turkish army came but slowly, we might be forced out again, and lose the plainsmen between Deraa and Damascus, in whose hands our final victory lay. A nice calculation, if hardly a fresh one, but on the whole the arguments were still against taking Deraa. Again we had to put off our friends with excuses within their comprehension."

Lawrence and the Arab leadership are careful not to take their eye off the prize despite assurances and persuasions to strike now. It's too tempting sometimes to settle a job before it is finally complete. During World War II, Roosevelt demanded unconditional surrender from the Germans despite heavy opposition among his own commanders and allies, who preferred the simpler solution of a quick surrender. He knew the value of not giving up just short of the finishing line.

In customer service, the less emotionally intelligent person tends to over-promise, which inevitably leads to unreasonably high expectations, under-performance and the consequent ruin of long-term prospects and relationships. People over-promise because they become desperate and short-sighted. Negative emotions like greed and fear get the better of them and the real goal goes out the window. Most people are scared by the future. The future is too uncertain so we grab the 'now' with both hands. The old proverb says that: "a bird in the hand is worth two in the bush" but that's not always true. Sometimes you need to hold your nerve and hold out for something better.

The emotionally intelligent person is true to himself and to others. He is not a victim of hearsay and fortune. He is able to put off present gain in favour of future benefit and to do that requires stoicism, self-belief, subtlety and people skills. Like Lawrence, the superior leader keeps cool and does what's best in the group's long term interests. He shows us that the good guy does win if he keeps faith with the strategy and vision.

117. Say 'Yes' First and Work Out How to Do It Later

Upon news of Allenby smashing the Turkish line in Palestine, Lawrence flies over to headquarters to hear the next stage of the plan and request RAF assistance in Jordan.

> "The Air chiefs turned on me and asked if our landing-grounds were good enough for a Handley-Page with full load. I had seen the big machine once in its shed, but unhesitatingly said 'Yes' though they had better send an expert over with me in the Bristols to-morrow and make sure. He might be back by noon, and the Handley come at three o'clock. Salmond got up: That's all right, Sir, we'll do the necessary.' I went out and breakfasted."

One characteristic of great employees and companies is that they have a healthy attitude towards stepping outside comfort zones to aid growth. This is exemplified by a default position of 'yes, we can' rather than the all too easy 'no, we've never done that before.' Having a natural 'yes' disposition is not the same as over-promising. It is about showing flexibility and confidence with clients and colleagues. If a request or idea is not feasible then that will be discovered in due course, but why say something can't be done if you haven't first tried?

The basic truth behind the 'yes' disposition is that it is simply more realistic to be positive, than taking a more deceptive negative stance. Effective people enjoy new projects and they take pride in the fact that they are there to serve, to satisfy people's requirements, to learn and to add value. You don't have to make a song and dance about your ability to do something but you do need to give a firm answer quickly and then quietly look for ways to overcome the objections, rules and obstacles that present themselves. In this way you keep expectations reasonable and perhaps even surprise people when your task succeeds.

118. True Understanding Comes Only from Experience

Back at camp, Lawrence presents the men with the new British aircraft and regales them with news of Allenby's victories. When enemy planes then hove into view Lawrence decides that in this case, caution is the better part of valour.

> "Meanwhile it was breakfast time with a smell of sausage in the air. We sat round, very ready: but the watcher on the broken tower yelled 'Aeroplane up', seeing one coming over from Deraa. Our Australians, scrambling wildly to their yet-hot machines, started them in a moment. Ross Smith, with his observer, leaped into one, and climbed like a cat up the sky. After him went Peters, while the third pilot stood beside the D.H.g and looked hard at me.
>
> I seemed not to understand him. Lewis guns, scarfe mountings, sights, rings which turned, vanes, knobs which rose and fell on swinging parallel bars; to shoot, one aimed with this side of the ring or with that, according to the varied speed and direction of oneself and the enemy. I had been told the theory, could repeat some of it: but it was in my head, and rules of action were only snares of action till they had run out of the empty head into the hands, by use. No: I was not going up to air-fight, no matter what caste I lost with the pilot. He was an Australian, of a race delighting in additional risks, not an Arab to whose gallery I must play."

We saw in Lessons 38 & 53 how leaders ought to set the example by demonstrating noesis, that is, intuitive knowledge as opposed to book-based learning. Repeated practice creates automaticity, whereby you do things without consciously thinking about them, like speaking a language fluently or riding a bicycle. The root of this distinction lies in the difference between a person's declarative and procedural memory. Declarative memory is an ability to recall facts like a person's name or birthday, whereas procedural memory is used in practising skills. Lawrence is careful not to confuse the two and bite off more than he can chew by rashly attempting to fly a plane into battle when he was not qualified or required to do so. He knew that explicit knowledge is good, but real understanding is better.

The title of this lesson comes from Leonardo da Vinci, whom we also mentioned in Lesson 38. One of the reasons for da Vinci's universal genius was the environment in which he grew up. His father was a government official who never spent much time with his son and Leonardo didn't meet his mother until much later in life. As such, his childhood was a solitary one in which he enjoyed great amounts of time to play and observe the world for what it was. It was this undirected freedom which allowed Leonardo to experiment and begin on a course to figuring out much of the structure of the world and the laws of nature. He must have known first-hand that experience is the mother of wisdom. Richard Feynman, the legendary teacher and physics genius, shared a similar enlightened upbringing and constantly stressed this fact.

'I learned very early the difference between knowing the name of something and knowing something.' ~ Richard Feynman

119. If You Challenge People, They Grow

Finally, with the help of the British, Lawrence and the Arabs chase down and massacre the last of the Turkish Fourth Army outside Daraa. On the cusp of victory, the masses retire to the camp at Kiswe.

> "The movement and cross-currents of so many crowded minds drove me about, restlessly, like themselves. In the night my colour was unseen. I could walk as I pleased, an unconsidered Arab: and this finding myself among, but cut off from, my own kin made me strangely alone. Our armoured-car men were persons to me, from their fewness and our long companionship; and also in their selves, for these months unshieldedly open to the flaming sun and bullying wind had worn and refined them into individuals. In such a mob of unaccustomed soldiery, British, Australian and Indian, they went as strange and timid as myself; distinguished also by grime, for with weeks of wearing their clothes had been moulded to them by sweat and use and had become rather integuments than wrappings."

As soldiers must, the British contingent — epitomised by Lawrence, have stepped out of a huge comfort zone by joining the revolt in the desert. Comfort zones are areas where people comfortably operate without risk. People generally dread stepping out of comfort zones because it can cause stress, humiliation and even death. Yet the value of doing this lies in the fact that, if something does not kill you, it makes you stronger. You may be broken temporarily, but you rebuild yourself stronger. You become reshaped, you grow thicker skin and you learn new skills. Trying new things is difficult but it cultivates your character and makes you a more effective person.

Richard Branson is the embodiment of this spirit. He is famous not just for being a billionaire but for trying to fly around the world in hot air balloons and similar breakneck stunts. Through his thirst for adventure and risks he has moulded himself into a formidable businessman and extraordinary individual.

> 'Adversity has the effect of eliciting talents, which in prosperous circumstances would have lain dormant.' ~ Horace

120. Say It in Ten Words or Less

When Damascus is conquered and settled, General Allenby arrives in pomp from Palestine to be greeted by the new Arab government.

> "When I got back to the hotel crowds were besetting it, and at the door stood a grey Rolls-Royce, which I knew for Allenby's. I ran in and found him there with Clayton and Cornwallis and other noble people. In ten words he gave his approval to my having impertinently imposed Arab Governments, here and at Deraa, upon the chaos of victory. He confirmed the appointment of Ah' Riza Rikabi as his Military Governor, under the orders of Feisal, his Army Commander, and regulated the Arab sphere and Chauvel's."

Allenby says what he has to say in only ten words and this is a good rule to work by. Equivocating like a politician who rambles on trying to cover himself on both sides, is a weak and dishonest way to communicate. Decisive people give a straight answer one way or the other and they don't sit on the fence. The German architect Ludwig Mies van der Rohe coined the phrase, 'less is more' and this attitude can be applied to many aspects of life and work. Rather than heaping on word after word when speaking to someone, a simple answer will usually suffice if you truly understand the situation. Verbosity often belies incompetence.

Ten words is a comfortable chunk to say whatever needs to be said at critical points. It is a useful constraint to work within because it forces you to be clear and to cut out unnecessary information. Like a tweet or a text, it gets to the heart of the matter.

As we have seen throughout this book, simplicity and clarity are the keys to quality, and if the insurgent entrepreneur can weave this philosophy into his or her business then they can build and command a winning organisation and campaign, against the odds, just as Lawrence did.

> 'Brevity is the soul of wit.' ~ Shakespeare, *Hamlet*

Epilogue

"*Damascus had not seemed a sheath for my sword, when I landed in Arabia: but its capture disclosed the exhaustion of my main springs of action. The strongest motive throughout had been a personal one, not mentioned Here, but present to me, I think, every hour of these two years. Active pains and joys might fling up, like towers, among my days: but, refluent as air, this hidden urge reformed, to be the persisting element of life, till near the end. It was dead, before we reached Damascus.*

Next in force had been a pugnacious wish to win the war: yoked to the conviction that without Arab help England could not pay the price of winning its Turkish sector. When Damascus fell, the eastern war—probably the whole war--drew to an end.

Then I was moved by curiosity. 'Super Flumina Babylonis', read as a boy, had left me longing to feel myself the node of a national Movement. We took Damascus, and I feared. More than three arbitrary days would have quickened in me a root of authority.

There remained historical ambition, insubstantial as a motive by itself. I had dreamed, at the city school in Oxford, of hustling into form, while I lived, the new Asia which time was inexorably bringing upon us. Mecca was to lead to Damascus; Damascus to Anatolia, and afterwards to Bagdad; and then there was Yemen. Fantasies, these will seem, to such as are able to call my beginning an ordinary effort."

Index

Numbers refer to <u>lessons</u>

Alexander the Great 42, 74, 75

Allegiances 21, 22, 93

Adversity 32, 51, 85, 96, 101, 119

Advertising copy 63, 120

Aesop 83

Allen, James 107

Asians 60

Assange, Julian 108

Assertiveness 55, 116

Attraction 105, 106, 107, 113

Autonomy 72, 98

Bandler, Richard 53, 95

Bernays, Edward 105

Blogging 27, 89

Branson, Richard 44, 64, 74, 94, 119

Bolivar, Simon 7

Buffett, Warren 40

Caesar, Julius 43, 52, 53, 74, 91

Camels 69

Character 110, 119

China 39, 84

Churchill, Winston 19, 35, 47, 104

Clausewitz, Carl von 32, 75

Clothes 102

Comfort zones 51, 101, 117, 119

Community 45, 79, 105, 106

Conflict 86, 93

Confucius 39, 109

Conservatism 100, 112

Controversy 63, 71

Courage 18, 30, 51, 54, 56, 95, 101, 110, 111, 116

Creative destruction 36, 80

Creativity 17, 50

Crisis 15, 101

Culture 13, 19, 49, 97, 106, 112

Cyrus the Great 43, 74

Da Vinci, Leonardo 38, 103, 118

Delegating 39, 50, 53, 79

Diathetic 42, 43

Discipline 16, 25, 83, 98

Disraeli, Benjamin 44, 87

Drucker, Peter 35, 73, 114

Economic moat 40

Einstein, Albert 60, 86

Emerson, Ralph Waldo 107

Emotional intelligence 12, 35, 43, 44, 60, 61, 62, 81, 104, 105, 110, 116

Espirit de corps 91

Equivocation 120

Face loss 16

Failure 16, 96, 101

Ferdinand of Aragon 82

Feynman, Richard 118

Foch, Ferdinand 32

Ford, Henry 11, 50

Formlessness 10, 35, 58

Freedom 56, 98, 112

Freud, Sigmund 105

Galton, Francis 94

Gates, Bill 15

Gandhi, Mohandas 56, 86

Google 59, 72

Gore-Tex 72

Grinder, John 53, 95

Guerrilla 69, 70, 72, 73, 75

Guevara, Che 75

Hacking 67

Hardship 51, 85, 96

Hemingway, Ernest 30

History 42, 88, 107, 109, 112

Hitler 8

Holenstein, Elmar 97

Hopper, Grace 95

Horace 119

Hubris 52, 58, 61, 79

Ideology 106

Incentives 9, 72

Intellectual property 67

Internal competition 92, 108

Internet 27, 41, 71, 89

Intuition 60, 99, 118

Inventor's paradox 34, 80

Isolation 50, 61, 79, 94, 100, 114

Jack of all trades 14, 101

Jihadism 68

Jobs, Steve 40, 80, 105

Jung, Carl 2

Korzybski, Alfred 37, 52, 61

Law of Requisite Variety ... 73

Less is more 103, 120

Lincoln, Abraham 92, 93

Logical fallacy 18, 97

Lollapalooza effect 113

Machiavelli, Nicolo 11, 12, 25, 28, 38, 53, 74, 82, 115

Manifesto 64

Market share 33, 52

Map and territory 37, 52, 61

Mehrabian, Albert 104

Memory 118

Meritocracy 29, 39

Metaphor 69

Mies van der Rohe, Ludwig 120

Mill, John Stuart 110

Milton Model 65, 66, 104

Misdirection 58, 104, 111, 113

Monopolistic competition ... 20, 36

Munger, Charlie 32, 113

Napoleon 75, 91, 106

Negotiation 22, 57, 61, 65, 66, 103, 104, 113

Nelson, Horatio 110

Niche 5, 33, 70, 75, 98

Nietzsche, Friederich 21, 42, 73

NLP 31, 37, 53, 65, 78, 95, 113

Noesis 38, 53, 118

Non-price competition 20, 36

Nostalgia 68, 84, 88

Obstacles 32, 51, 100

Opinions 115

Optimism 23, 99, 117

Pareto efficiency 47

Peters, Tom 39

Pink, Dan 72

Plutarch 107

Powell, Colin 18, 94

Pragmatism 8, 50, 95, 101, 112, 115

Problem solving 34, 86, 117

Promises 12, 48, 116, 117

Propaganda 43, 104, 105

Rationality 105, 117

REM sleep 34

Requisite variety 47, 112

Resources 11, 21, 47, 51, 87

Rhetoric 63, 103, 106

Rhodes, Cecil 85

Risks 77, 100, 118, 119

Roosevelt, Franklin D 116

Scepticism 37, 94, 95

Schumpeter, Joseph 36

Shakespeare 9, 112, 120

Socrates 42

Soundbites 103

Spies 67, 79

Stoicism 87, 116

Subconscious 34, 38, 104, 105, 107, 113

Subtlety 46, 104, 105, 113

Sun Zi 10, 20, 67, 111

Surprise 63, 80, 117

Sykes-Picot Agreement 108

Synchronicity 2, 107

Teaching 41, 109, 110

Teamwork 51, 54, 83, 97, 115

Tennyson, Alfred 82

Thales 42

Thatcher, Margaret 93

Thinking ahead 11, 21, 50, 76, 111, 112, 116

Thirty-Six Stratagems 22, 58, 68, 84, 108

Time management 17, 34, 50

Tipping point 85

Total War 75

Vision 6, 23, 63, 99, 106, 107, 111, 116

Voltaire 15, 110

Washington, George 7

Weekly communiqués 6

Welch, Jack 40

Wellington 75

Westerners 60

Win-win 21, 22, 67, 66

Wild people 90

Winging it 101, 117

Wisdom of Crowds 94, 111, 115

Wishful thinking 48, 61, 79, 88

Word of mouth 70, 85, 113

Xenophon 42